Penny Loafers & Bobby Pins

Penny Loafers & Bobby Pins

Tales and Tips from Growing Up in the '50s and '60s

Susan Sanvidge
Diane Sanvidge Seckar
Jean Sanvidge Wouters
Julie Sanvidge Florence

Wisconsin Historical Society Press

Published by the Wisconsin Historical Society Press
Publishers since 1855

© 2010 by the State Historical Society of Wisconsin

For permission to reuse material from *Penny Loafers & Bobby Pins*
(ISBN 978-0-87020-446-3), please access www.copyright.com or contact the
Copyright Clearance Center, Inc. (CCC), 222 Rosewood Drive, Danvers, MA
01923, 978-750-8400. CCC is a not-for-profit organization that provides licenses and
registration for a variety of users.

wisconsin history.org

Photos and illustrations are from the authors' collections unless otherwise credited.

Printed in the United States of America

Designed by Sue Ellibee
Cover illustrations by Linda Takaha

14 13 12 11 10   1 2 3 4 5

Library of Congress Cataloging-in-Publication Data

Penny loafers & bobby pins : tales and tips from growing up in the 50s and 60s / Susan Sanvidge ... [et al.].
p. cm.
Includes index.
ISBN 978-0-87020-446-3 (pbk. : alk. paper) 1. Cookery, American—Midwestern style. 2. Cookery—Wisconsin. 3.
Handicraft—Wisconsin—Miscellanea. 4. Oshkosh (Wis.)—Social life and customs—20th century. I. Sanvidge, Susan.
TX715.2.M53P46 2010
641.59775—dc22

                    2009048004

∞The paper used in this publication meets the minimum requirements of the American National Standard for
Information Sciences—Permanence of Paper for Printed Library Materials, ANSI Z39.48-1992.

To our mother, Helen Noffke Sanvidge,
who said, "Write more stories."

vi

Contents

Introduction   X

The Early Fifties 1

The First Houses That Dad Built (for Us) 2

The House We Grew Up in Most 4 *How to Play Seven Steps around the House 8*

Red Rover and the Big Storm 9 *What Happened to My Ring? 11*

"Why Don't You Kids Go Outside and Play?" 12
*How to Bundle Up in Twelve Easy Steps 14   How to Play Steal the Bacon (on Skates) 16
How to Play Seven-Up: A One-Person Ball Game 18*

Grandma Noffke 19 *How to Make Grandma Noffke's "German Potato Salad" Cure 22
From the Kitchen: Grandma Noffke's Apple Butter 23*

"Look It Up!" 24

Pink Peonies on the Dining Room Table 26 *How to Make More African Violets 29*

Home Permanents 30 *How to Get Bouncy Fifties Hair with Pin Curls 31*

Oom-pah-pah, Oom-pah-pah 33

St. Mary's Grade School 35 *Sign My Autograph Book, Please 37
How to Make a Chinese Jump Rope 41   Jump Rope Rhymes We Have Known 42
How to Make a Folded Paper Fortune Teller 44*

Polio 48

Best Friends 49 *How to Play Hopscotch 54
How to Write with Palmer Method Penmanship 56*

The Legendary Cottage at Three Lakes 57 *From the Kitchen: Apple Fritters 63*

The Late Fifties 65

The Early Sixties 117

Dad came back from World War II and married Mom, and the four of us were born in Oshkosh, Wisconsin, between 1948 and 1958. Oshkosh is where we rode tricycles, twirled hula hoops, and opened new boxes of crayons on the first day of school. The sign outside Oshkosh said POPULATION 41,084 back then, but when we went downtown, we always ran into somebody we knew.

In the fifties, sleek Mixmasters were replacing rusty eggbeaters, and new pressure-cookers blew their tops in kitchens all over town. There were kids everywhere, and new ranch-style houses filled vacant lots (our dad was building some of those houses). Turquoise Studebakers and dusty-rose Chevy BelAirs with flamboyant fins and lots of chrome replaced dark prewar cars. Cameras took color snapshots instead of black-and-white. We wore red canvas tennis shoes with lemon yellow shorts, and bright blue popsicles melted down our chins. It seemed like there was color everywhere, except on the television sets that were being delivered to more and more living rooms.

By the beginning of the sixties, television had connected us to the world outside of our town. The Walt Disney show that we liked to watch on Sunday nights (before Ed Sullivan's "really big 'shew'") became *Walt Disney's Wonderful World of Color*. It opened with a song, "Color . . . color . . . the world is a carousel of color. Wonderful, wonderful color, color-color-color . . .," that made us *insane* watching it on our black-and-white TV.

Sister after sister, we scribbled in our workbooks at St. Mary's School and pondered the mystery of nuns. And sister after sister, we grew up.

Our days passed in a kaleidoscope of swing sets and skates, Tiny Tears and Barbie dolls, Tinkertoys and potholder weaving, jump ropes and gum wrapper chains, pin curls and home permanents, adventures in our bus and days at the cottage. We went from poodle skirts and Buster Brown socks to A-line dresses and nylons. All along we were learning things we can't forget (no matter how hard we try), from Mom and Dad, and our grandmas and grandpas who all lived nearby. Mom's "First do your work, then play" is etched in our brains—along with "Don't sit on the concrete, you'll get piles," from one of our grandmas.

Our toys are in the attic now, and this is what we remember.

—*Susan*

It's 1958 and we're in the backyard, next to the swing set, with our neighborhood playmates and our hula hoops. That's Diane at the top, making a Picture Face. Next row down is Susie on the left and Patsy Lux on the right, both with their hair in pin curls. (It must have been a Saturday.) In front at the left is Mary Lou Lux next to Jean, who is holding baby sister Julie.

The Early Fifties

"First comes love, then comes marriage, and along comes (Helen) with a baby carriage"—and I was in it. For almost two years, I was the pampered darling; the big cheese; the apple of my grandparents' eyes . . .—*Susan*

Dad in the doorway of the first house he ever built (very maturely sticking out his tongue): our family's first house. Grandma and Grandpa Sanvidge have come to take a look at it.

The First Houses That Dad Built (for Us)

When Mom and Dad married in 1947, they moved into the first house Dad ever built, a sweet little house with a bay window on Powers Street in Oshkosh. Dad had worked as a carpenter for a while before the war, and when he was in the army he had taken a correspondence course in carpentry. This was a good thing to do, because after the war many people needed houses. We lived in this house for only two years. Somebody wanted to buy the house, and Dad . . . sold it.

I was one and a half when we moved out of the house on Powers into a one-car garage Dad built on a Bowen Street lot across the street from Grandma and Grandpa Noffke's. We lived in the dark little garage from late May to early September, while Dad was building our new house. Dad made a big screen to fit the garage door opening (not too private, but breezy), and Mom made green gingham curtains. Our bathroom . . . was across the street at Grandma's. There was a cream-colored cupboard in the garage decorated with a border of red tulips and green leaves. I must have fixed on this as the prettiest

thing in the dark little garage. Later, whenever a teacher would tell us to decorate something, the first thing I always thought of was red tulips with green leaves on a yellow background.

By September, we were living in a brand-new white brick house, with a bathroom of our very own. Diane was born the next spring, and soon after, Mom was pregnant with Jean. We hadn't lived there one year when Clifford Jones rang our doorbell. He wanted to buy our house, and since Dad had already bought the lot next door . . .

I think this is where Mom "put her foot down" and kept us from Gypsy Life. She had barely put up the curtains, and she was not about to live in a garage with three little kids. This time Dad had to build the house first (it helped that the Joneses were willing to wait), and we moved into our next new house when it was done.

Mom's foot must have stayed down for a while. The next move would be in the early seventies.—*Susan*

That tiny garage is where we lived while Dad finished building our second house. There were a few old houses on the block, but many of the lots were empty at the time. By the early sixties, there would be a house on every lot.

The House We Grew Up in Most

By the end of 1952, we were living in our new-house-next-door, a three-bedroom ranch-style house with a two-car garage, and Dad had planted two skinny red maples (five or six leaves per tree) in the front yard. Our '49 Chevy was parked in the driveway, soon to be replaced with a natty charcoal gray '53 Buick. We were all set for Life in the Fifties.

I'll give you a tour. Let's start with the back door, because we use it the most. Take one step up onto the concrete stoop, past the Fahrnwald milkbox (I'll take that milk in), and in the back door. Those steps ahead of you go down to the basement. We have a playroom in one corner down there—it even has a door to close, so we can make a lot of noise. That cabinet behind the open back door is completely stuffed with jackets, mittens, and scarves. I wouldn't open it if I were you.

This "trivet" was on our kitchen wall.

Turn right, step up, and here's our big kitchen with swirly dark green linoleum that Mom waxes and strips, waxes and strips. Dad built our yellow linoleum-covered table. Yes, it is big enough for a Ping-Pong game, but we have to drag all those heavy chrome and red vinyl chairs out of the way first. Mom always says, "Be careful, you'll make marks on the floor!" Out the double windows over the table you can see our backyard: swing set, clotheslines, Dad's vegetable garden (Is that a *ripe* tomato?), and Mom's Sweet William and Sweet Alyssum (which does not smell sweet) around the trellis.

The black iron things next to the clock on that wallpapered wall are for decoration. They are called trivets. Since Mom put that matching Pennsylvania Dutch wallpaper on the face of the clock, it's been easier to check the Timex watches we got for Christmas.

In the cupboards next to the stove are what's left of Mom's Blue Ridge china with the apples on it, and lots and lots of ripped-open cereal boxes (minus the prizes). A black-and-white Mixmaster is under that quilted cover by the canisters. Mom puts trailing ivy and the fragile, pretty things inherited from her grandma on those little curved shelves, so she has something to look at instead of the neighbor's siding while she's doing dishes.

I should put this milk in the fridge. (Oooh, there's *pudding* under the wax paper.) That big white thing next to the fridge is "iron-ically" called a mangle. It's for ironing big flat things like sheets and tablecloths.

We like to run and slide in our socks down this long red linoleum hallway. Sometimes Mom even asks us to do this, to buff the wax. That's a built-in gun cabinet on your left (that's why it has a lock), and this dark brown room is our dad's office. We call it the den. Mom's rose pink bridesmaid dress and Dad's old army uniform are in that closet—it has all the best clothes for playing "dress-up."

The door with the knocker that says HONI SOIT QUI MAL Y PENSE ("Shamed be he who thinks evil of it")—that's the bathroom. Dad's manicure scissors are "hidden" under the towels on the top shelf of this built-in cabinet. These are the only scissors we can ever find in our house, and Dad says there will be "hell to pay" if we don't put them back. Check out the pink contact paper with the fish on it, the hairbrushes we got from the Fuller Brush man, and the black bobby pins scattered everywhere.

That's a linen closet at the end of the hallway, and to the right is Mom and Dad's bedroom. Their dark mahogany bedroom set is "Duncan Phyfe–style." They got it from Grandma and Grandpa as a wedding present, and the bathroom door knocker came with this white bedspread. If we look on the very top shelf of

Mom and Dad's closet in December, we can sneak a peak at Christmas presents.

Across the hall is the bedroom that Diane and Jeanie and I share. I sleep with Diane in the double bed. (It was somebody's leftover furniture.) One of us is always saying, "You're on my side!" (Mom won't let us draw a line on the sheets), and then Dad says, "You girls better pipe down!" Jeanie gets to sleep all by herself in the youth bed with little fences on the sides. The modernistic blond chest of drawers with big gold dented-in knobs inspired Mom to "blond" our different-color beds. She used a kit with a rubber comb to fake the streaks. So both beds match now, and our new ruffly bedspreads do, too. We used to have a faded red chenille bedspread on the big bed, but we ate most of the chenille.

A word about the walls: Be careful not to bump them, or you'll scrape your skin off. There is sand in the plaster for "texture"—and maybe so we will keep our hands off the wall (unless we have an itch).

Let's go back down the hall to the living room at the other end. The gray stones on the fireplace are Lannon stone. We think the green woolly carpeting and the big flowers and leaves on the curtains make it feel like being outdoors in here, and our favorite thing in the room is in front of the wall with the red wallpaper and country road pictures: our new television! The repairman had to replace too many tubes or *something* in our first television set—the picture kept rolling and rolling, and there was lots of "snow."

Mom putting the "woman's touch" on our house

The couch and matching chair—we call that color cocoa brown—have hard little loops (feel them) that scratch you if you're wearing shorts. For a while we had a tan leather chair that had buttons on the back that got twisted in our hair, and then the leather started ripping, so it's gone now. That chair with the loopy rust-colored upholstery and wood arms is another scratchy thing to sit on. It's not *too* surprising that we usually sit on the floor to watch TV, is it? Or that most of us have eczema?

The oval picture above the rust chair is called "The Sacred Heart." We think it's here to remind us to be good, and it *is* right next to the front hall closet with the Good Coats, Easter Hats, and Good Purses—the clothes we wear to church. Before I open the front door, look down at the floor here. It's linoleum, but doesn't it look like little bricks?

Let's go outside and look at Mom's climbing rose bush. It's just loaded with flowers, and Mom's out there taking pictures.—*Susan*

From left to right: Susan, Jean, Diane, and our neighbor, Sharon Dietrich, in front of Mom's climbing rose bush, the envy of the neighborhood

How to Play Seven Steps around the House

First of all, to play Seven Steps around the House, you need a house that doesn't have pretty flowerbeds around the sides that would most likely get trampled playing this game, or you'll get yelled at. Our cottage up north, which was small with only a limited area of tough and forgiving evergreens skirting it, was perfect for this game. Seven Steps was a great game to play when it was too cold to go swimming.

Choose a person to be "It." (Most likely this is the person whose idea it was to play the game.) Choose a spot to be "Home"—a front stoop is a good place. Hopefully you've rounded up a bunch of other kids with nothing better to do to be the "Players."

The Players get seven free steps (always going in one direction) to begin the game. The It person can move in either direction. The object of the game is for the It person to get completely around the house at least once and to catch the Players in motion. When a Player is caught in motion he or she has to go back to Home and start over. The first Player to get back Home without getting caught is the winner, the game is over, and the winner is It for the next game.—*Jean*

Red Rover and the Big Storm

In the early fifties, Dad converted a retired city bus into an early form of RV/camper and named it "The Rover" by putting stick-on letters on its sides—but we all called it "Red Rover" because it was red. For seven summers, we spent our weekends traveling from trout stream to trout stream all over Wisconsin. (Dad loved trout fishing.) We had many adventures in Red Rover, so many adventures that our parents came to the conclusion that a cottage would be a much safer option.

One hot and humid Sunday afternoon, Dad was at the wheel of Red Rover driving us back to Oshkosh. It was Jeanie's turn to sit on the big milk can (our water supply) next to Dad, and she was holding on tight to the railing. Behind Dad, Diane and I sat next to Mom on the old bus seats Dad had left in. We were waiting impatiently for our turn to sit on the milk can, and our legs were sticking to the hot leather seats. Dad said something about the sky, and when we twisted around to look out the windows, the sky looked all dirty.

A big howling wind started up. It was blowing the trees around—even the grass was swirling—and Dad was having a hard time keeping our big, boxy bus on the road. He had to pull over onto the crunchy gravel shoulder. There was a ditch next to us, and Dad knew we couldn't stay there.

"The Rover" (parked in our driveway here) had a silver top, but the rest of it was red, so we always called it "Red Rover." Left to right: Diane, Susan, and Jean wearing cowboy hats on top of scarves, with our little neighbor, Howie Jones. Above us is the back of the refrigerator, a genuine icebox that required a big block of ice.

Our bus was as big as a billboard and the wind was rocking it back and forth, back and forth. The bus felt like it was going to tip over any minute, and we were scared to the point of giggling hysteria. While our mom and dad were frantically trying to figure out what to do, we were running around, alternately screaming and laughing. It was like a ride at the fair! Then the elastic in Jeanie's pants popped—and they fell down. We thought this was *so* hilarious and scrambled all over the rocking bus, trying to find Jeanie's popped-out elastic.

Dad remembered a nearby road cut into a hill that would block the wind. While Mom gathered us up, Dad slowly pulled back onto the highway. We sat out the storm sheltered by that hill. The wind roared, the grass swirled—and big trees were going down all around us. (I had to ask our mother about this crucial part of the story, because what my sisters and I have always remembered most is Jean's elastic popping.)

After a long time, the air was finally quiet, and we were safe. Dad started up the bus again. Road after road was blocked by huge fallen trees (we remember this part very well), and he had to turn the bus around again and again to try another route. Some roads were blocked with big broken-off branches, and Dad worked with other drivers to clear them. It took us a very long time to get back home to Oshkosh.—*Susan*

After the storm: Dad and Mom, Jean (in different pants, which are on backwards), Susan, and Diane

Postscript: Just last year, this thought slid into my head: Jean's elastic would still be in her pants.

What Happened to My Ring?

We all got adjustable birthstone rings at Woolworth's. Mine was gold with a pretty amber stone. (My birthday is in March. Shouldn't I have picked aquamarine?) I was so happy I stopped biting my nails. I turned the ring around and around and slipped it on and off my finger a hundred times.

That weekend we took a trip in Red Rover. Dad pulled off the highway, opened a rusty gate, and drove down a bumpy dirt road through a pasture with tall weeds and lots of dried cow pies to our parking spot on the Wolf River. Mom set up a cot outside for us to sit on and sent us out to play. Susie accidentally dropped her ring through one of the hand holes in the cot. We searched through the grass and couldn't find it. That's when Susie came up with her great idea:

"So what happened to my ring?"

"Diane. Drop your ring through the same hole. We can watch it fall and that's where my ring will be."

We found Susie's ring, but mine was lost forever.—*Diane*

Mea culpa, mea culpa, mea maxima *culpa! Will you ever forgive me?*—*Susan*

"Why Don't You Kids Go Outside and Play?"

Mom needs *just-one-quiet-cup-of-coffee*, and we need to yell!

When snow was piled up around our back door in its usual drift, and being cooped up in the house was getting too much for everyone, it was time to bundle up and head outside with our "flying saucer." We almost never used our sled with the red steel runners because no matter what kind of snow we had, it wasn't the right kind for that sled. The flying saucer (its real name was Sno-Coaster, but nobody called it that), a shallow metal bowl with leather handles and holes for a rope, was the most fun in the snow. We could pull each other with a rope, spin it in circles, slide down snow hills, give it a push on ice—and it worked on *any* kind of snow.

We played for hours in the snow. On sunny days, we could hardly see when we came inside. We made snow angels, snow forts, snowmen, and slides out of snowdrifts. The annual January thaw usually melted all the snow into water, and our low backyard was always flooded. Then the weather would get cold again and make us our own backyard ice rink (which included the Krause and Dietrich backyards behind ours). We could ice skate right out our back door!

Pretty soon having a pair of ice skates was right up there in importance with shoes and boots. We started out with two-runner kiddie skates and Uncle Jimmy's old black hockey skates. Soon we had brand-new white figure skates, and the neighbor kids were out there skating, too. The Krauses' clothesline poles, sticking up out of the ice, marked the centerline for games of Steal the Bacon. We had to skate around the stubs of plants and avoid spots of dry grass, and occasionally we slammed into a garage, but you couldn't beat the location.

In early spring, our skating rink melted into a multi-backyard puddle, with drowned angleworms floating everywhere. One year we had a great idea: Dad could use those worms for fishing! So we gathered a big (dirtless) pail of angleworms (drowned) and put it in the (spring-warmed) garage. It didn't take much to make

Dad gag, and this was more than enough. We never did *that* again.

We didn't have to be asked to go outside in summer. The screen door was banging open and shut all day long. We ate peas, carrots (rubbed on the grass to get the dirt off), peppers, green beans, and tomatoes straight from the garden, and one year we planted our very own small garden behind the garage. We played in dirt piles, our sandbox, and caught baby rabbits on empty lots. (We kept two wild rabbits as pets for a while: Peppy

Our sturdy swing set (which Dad hired someone to build) was so popular in the neighborhood that Dad took out a special insurance policy. Left to right: Diane, Jean, Susan.

and Pokey. We soon found out why Pokey was so lethargic: he was sick, and then he died. Peppy, who loved white clover blossoms, was lively and feisty—and always trying to escape. One day we took Peppy out to the backyard and let him go.)

We had jumping-off routines when we played on the swings. (*"J-Jump" meant it was my turn to jump and I would pray that I didn't split my pants.—Jean*) A blanket over the side bar of the swing set made a tent, and a blanket in the shade was a good place to play on a hot day. All summer long we played baseball after supper on Grandma and Grandpa Noffke's big lawn with the neighbor kids. We used a Wiffle ball with its skinny yellow plastic bat, until Dad bought us our own softball and a black wooden bat. (We never did break Grandma and Grandpa's picture window.)

We played outside until the streetlights came on. That was our signal to come home.—*Susan and Jean*

How to Bundle Up in Twelve Easy Steps

Believe you me (as Mom would say), we couldn't just throw on any old jacket and dash outside to play in the billowing snow and biting cold of a Wisconsin winter. "Bundle up! It's cold outside!" says Mom, as we head to the back door closet for . . .

1. Snow pants. (These were thick and heavy "wool coats for our legs," which came with our equally thick and heavy winter coats.) Pull them up and connect the straps. You may need some help with the one that's dangling behind your back. Done? You may notice that your legs are now farther apart.

2. Boots. Pull on your rubber boots with the fur tops over your shoes and zip them up. Oof! You can't bend over too well in your thick snow pants! Be sure to have a wall nearby to fall on. Make sure your snow pants don't get caught in the zipper.

3. Oops! You forgot to go to the bathroom.

4. Repeat step number one.

5. Put on your coat. Button it all the way to the top. You don't want the snow to get in.

6. Put on your hat. Make sure it's one that ties under your chin, so it won't fall off. Snow might get on your head!

7. Put on your mitt—— Wait, the mitten string has to go through the coat sleeves first . . .

8. Take off your coat. (Find a Kleenex to wipe your sweaty face.)

9. Put the mitten string through the sleeves and put on your coat. "Button up! It's cold outside!"

10. Put your mittens on. This may take a while because sometimes those strings get stretched so long you can't reach the mitten. (You might want to stand next to that wall again.) If you twirl the string you might be able to catch that mitten down there . . .

11. Yes, you can say "I'm hot" in a pitiful whine.

12. Waddle over to Mom so she can tie your scarf over your face, real tight, so the snow doesn't get in. You don't want the snow to get in!

Now—if you can move—you're all set for fun in the snow.

Oh no! It's time for lunch!—*Susan*

Diane, Jean, and Susan (who is wondering if Mom the photographer will notice that she is not wearing her scarf)

How to Play Steal the Bacon (on Skates)

If you have nothing better to do on a cold winter's day *and* you have access to a good-size patch of ice *and* you have a pair of ice skates *and* you have a group of friends who have ice skates *and* nothing better to do, you could play a game of Steal the Bacon. I'm not sure why it was called that when there was, unfortunately, no bacon involved whatsoever. The "bacon" could be a hat, mitten, scarf, or whatever you could find that wasn't needed to keep somebody warm and preferably something old so you wouldn't get yelled at if someone skated over it and ruined it.

1. If playing the game is your idea, or you're the biggest or oldest kid or you just like being in charge, you can declare yourself "the umpire." Start by dividing up the players into two teams. Try to be fair and even up the teams for size and ability.

2. Line the two teams up facing each other about fifteen feet apart (that's about the length-and-a-half of a Buick Roadmaster). Decide how many points it's going to take to win the game based on how much time you have to play.

3. Starting at the same end of each line, have the players count off so there are matching numbers for each line.

4. Place the "bacon" in the center between the two lines of players. When you have gotten out of the way, call out a number.

5. The players with matching numbers try to grab the "bacon" (hopefully without getting hit in the head by a skate blade) and race back to their team without getting tagged by the opposing player. A point is gained each time a player gets the "bacon" home safe to his or her team. The team that reaches the agreed-upon number of points is the winner.—*Jean*

Our friend and neighbor Patsy, trying to do a headstand on ice, in her skates. Can you tell this photo was not taken by a grownup? (We each got a Brownie camera for Christmas.)

How to Play Seven-Up: A One-Person Ball Game

You will need: a small rubber ball or tennis ball, a reasonably flat wall (siding makes this tricky, and it made our parents cranky)—and no one to play with.

7. Throw the ball against the wall and catch it. Do this seven times.

6. Throw the ball against the wall, let it bounce once, and catch it. Do this six times.

5. Bounce the ball on the ground five times (like dribbling a basketball).

4. Bounce the ball on the ground once, then bat it to the wall with your hand. Let it bounce once, and catch it. Do this four times.

3. Bounce the ball on the ground once, then bat it to the wall and catch it before it hits the ground. Do this three times.

2. Throw the ball against the wall from under your leg (yes, lift it). Let it bounce once and catch it. Do this two times.

1. Throw the ball against the wall, twirl around once, and catch the ball before it hits the ground. Do this once. (It's enough.)

If you make one teensy little mistake, you have to start all over again from the beginning.—*Susan*

Grandma Noffke

Grandma Noffke (born Marie Agnes Schroth) wore a thick wool Pendleton jacket that was gold-and-brown plaid, like her dishes. She was five-foot-seven, which was quite tall for women of her generation, with straight gray hair that used to be black, pulled back in a donut-shaped bun. When she was ready to go to sleep, she would put her hair in a braid down her back and wear a navy blue bathrobe with white piping. Her skin was always beautiful, quite darkly tanned (she loved working in her garden and spent winters in Florida), and it stayed smooth, even as she got older. She wore a black onyx ring with a little diamond set in the center, and her glasses were tortoiseshell. If you picture the fifties styles for Grandma types you can see that Grandma Noffke had her own style. Our dad always said he couldn't have gotten a better mother-in-law.

Grandma Noffke about to go work in her garden. Grandpa's business, Noffke Fuel (later Noffke Lumber), is in the background.

Grandma was a calm and competent person with a sense of humor, who got cross rather than mad, and living with Grandpa put this to the test. She did all the bookkeeping for Grandpa's business and worked in the office. (Later we found out that Grandma would alter the numbers she showed to Grandpa so he wouldn't think he had so much money to spend.) Lucille Degner worked as their live-in housekeeper during the weekdays. When Grandma had free time she worked along with Cile, and over the years they became more like sisters. Cile was like a relative to us, too, and she stayed on with Grandma and Grandpa her whole life.

Grandma Noffke was a believer in the book *Vermont Folk Medicine*, old-time cures, and wholesome food. Ring the door at Grandma's on Halloween and you would get a box of raisins. Mention that you have a sore throat and you might have to put up with "The German Potato Salad" Cure (which follows this story). If you coughed, you would be offered Grandma's home-brewed pine tar cough syrup.

In Florida, Grandma collected all types of seashells for us, and she gave us a book to identify them. She made us winter play jackets from Grandpa's old coats, flannel pajamas every year for Christmas, and one year she even made matching pajamas for our new dolls. She turned every scrap of leftover wool into huge braided rugs. Grandma was always doing something, but she never seemed to be rushed.

Surprisingly, Grandma had her eyes open for the latest trend. It was Grandma Noffke who introduced us to Fritos and brought us an orange-and-yellow-striped beach bag from Florida for our "itsy bitsy 'beginas.'" Our first hi-fi—a blue-and-white "pre-stereo" record player with one attached speaker—was a Christmas present from Grandma (halfway across her lawn, we already

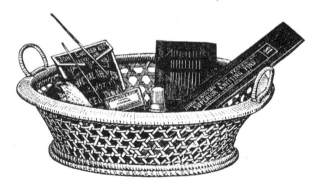

had enough wrapping off to see what it was). She gave us the first Bermuda shorts we'd ever heard of. They were tattersall—black and red lines on white, and they came with red belts and red polo shirts. Mom got a matching outfit, too. On one of my birthdays, Grandma gave me two pairs of store-bought pajamas. These were not ordinary pastel-and-flower-type pajamas; they were dark paisley flannel with wide cowl necks and the tops came to a pixielike point at the hem. The bottoms were pedal-pushers. One pair had bright red trim, the other gold. I loved them (but at first they would scare me when I woke up).

Grandma making the face

Grandma would say "Gosh oh fishhooks!" when something was funny or amazing. She was interested in our lives and very definitely a big part of our childhood. We all loved and admired her.

I have hands that look like Grandma's (same glove size, too), but Jean has her green thumb. Mom, Julie, and I all have Grandma's jawline. Every now and then, I catch myself in a facial expression, raised eyebrows and a Stan Laurel smile, that I know came from Grandma Noffke, because I actually feel like Grandma when it happens. I think it would be a good thing to *be* like Grandma Noffke all the time.—*Susan*

November 25, 2004: I saw Diane making Grandma's expression at Thanksgiving.

How to Make Grandma Noffke's "German Potato Salad" Cure

When we were gathering family recipes for our book *Apple Betty & Sloppy Joe*, Diane noticed the striking similarity between Grandma Noffke's infamous sore throat remedy and German potato salad. We asked our mom for the details, so you can try this at home.

Fry up about six strips of bacon (plus a few more to eat, because you know you will), but don't let the bacon strips allotted for the "cure" get too crisp. Meanwhile, soak a clean dishtowel in a bowl of plain white vinegar. When the bacon strips (for the cure) are cooked but still limp—and still *hot*—wring out the vinegar-soaked towel so it's not sopping wet and lay the hot bacon on the towel. Loosely roll up the vinegar-towel with the hot bacon inside, and loosely wrap a clean, dry (but not for long) dish towel around it. Make sure the bacon isn't *too* hot, and drape this lovely thing around the neck of your patient—who will never whine about a sore throat again.

Why the bacon? Our mom says it's there to produce heat (which creates warm vinegar fumes . . .). No guarantees!—*Susan*

Grandma Noffke's Apple Butter

Apple butter is darker, sweeter, thicker, and spicier than applesauce. There's no butter in it, as you'll soon find out, but like butter, it's good on bread—and great on toast (with butter *under* it). Grandma made apple butter for Mom and her brothers when they were growing up, but when Mom made it for us she left out the allspice.—*Susan*

Makes about a quart

Water
11 medium-size apples, pared and sliced (Macintosh are good.)
1 cup sugar
1 teaspoon cinnamon
½ teaspoon allspice

Put about ¼ cup of water in the bottom of a pan that has a tight-fitting cover, and add the pared, sliced apples. Cook over low heat—covered—until the apples are thoroughly cooked, stirring occasionally. The apples should be completely dissolved and the apple "soup" shouldn't look watery. While still on low heat, gradually stir in the sugar (so it melts into the apples), and then stir in the spices. (Our mother—who is notorious for skimping on spices—suggests that you put in only half of the spices and taste before putting in the other half.) Mom says you can put the apple butter into little jars and freeze it.

That's me, baby Jean, back when my birthday was April 24.

"Look It Up!"

When I was growing up and would ask my mom a million questions, she would say: "I don't know. Why don't you look it up?" Well, on one particular occasion, Mom got a taste of her own medicine . . .

When my oldest sister, Susan Marie Sanvidge, was born, Mom received or purchased (I'm not sure which, since I wasn't even a twinkle in my Dad's eye yet) a big, beautiful, pink moiré-covered baby book for the great occasion. *All* the pertinent information was carefully recorded: birthdate, time, height, weight, hair color, eye color, footprints, parents, grandparents, hospital, city, county, state, planet, and so on. For two years at least, Susie's every monumental event: first tooth, first word, first step . . . every precious moment was recorded.

Enter Diane, who came home from the hospital with the baby book the hospital provided for new parents. Again, all the pertinent information was carefully recorded. However, less of Diane's progress was recorded (perhaps due to less free time for Mom with a toddler and a baby to look after).

One year and one month later, along came me. With two very small toddlers and a newborn, Mom had her hands full. I also received a free baby book from the hospital, but not a word made it into that baby book—not even my name or birthdate.

When I was six years old (maybe seven or eight?), Grandma Sanvidge, who recorded all the family birthdates in her Bible, said to Mom, "I think you're celebrating Jeanie's birthday on the wrong day." Mom was stunned! She had always remembered my "birthday," April 24, as being near her dad's birthday, April 26. Totally embarrassed, she made up her mind to "look it up" as soon as she could. (Is this what started Mom saying "Look it up"?)

Grandma Noffke was in the hospital for an operation, and when Mom was visiting her, she checked the hospital records for my birthdate. To her shock and horror she found that my birthday was not April 24, but April 20!

Regardless of what day my parents celebrated my birthday, I know I was loved and cared for. I consider myself very blessed to have been born into the Sanvidge family . . . on whatever day I arrived.—*Jean*

Baby Girl Sanvidge
Date 4-20-51
Time 10:53 Pm.
Wt. 8# 9oz
Head 14"
Shoulders 15"
Chest 13½"
Abdomen 12"
Hips 11½"
Length 24"

Jean's "Baby Book," a 3 x 5 card. This is what was written and given to Mom from the hospital records. (*Oh no, Jean, your real name is "Baby Girl"!—Susan*)

Pink Peonies on the Dining Room Table

Very often we would walk across the street, past the big evergreen, across the big lawn, to Grandma and Grandpa Noffke's house. We always went in through the back screen porch, where Grandpa left his muddy boots next to vegetables brought in from Grandma's garden, and up four steps into a dark hallway with a row of built-in cabinets on one side. A refrigerator, holding Grandpa's stinky Limburger cheese, his beloved (stinky) kippersnacks, and glass milk bottles with a bulge on top holding thick yellow cream, was tucked into a niche at the end near a big square kitchen with white metal cabinets and dark red countertops. Grandma and Grandpa's bedroom, a rosy-tiled bathroom, and the stairs to the second floor opened off this hallway, too.

A heavy, golden-oak table with ornate chairs (Grandpa bought the set at an auction) almost filled the dining room. Peonies bloom only a short while in the summer, but it seemed like there was always a fragrant, drooping bouquet of shell pink peonies on that table. The living room walls were pale green swirling plaster, with chalky green tiles around a tidy, unused fireplace. In one corner was a squashy dark red upholstered chair next to a bookcase with family photos on top. Next to the up-to-date gold-brown couch across the room was a sturdy

Looking across Bowen Street at Grandma and Grandpa Noffke's house. Grandpa built the house, and Lester Grose, a fine mason and a longtime family friend, did the stonework. Later, when Dad was building houses, Lester was his mason.

wood chair with a needlepoint seat for our hefty Grandpa. A plant stand filled with pots and pots of African violets, all shades of purple and pink, and a few white ones, stood in front of a north-facing picture window overlooking the lawn. (This was the window we tried not to break when we played softball there, summer after summer.) Everything felt solid and like it had always been there, including the dark piece of furniture that was the first TV we ever saw. It had a screen about the size and shape of a Woolworth's fishbowl. Before we had our own television set, we would watch TV at Grandma and Grandpa's.

There were four rooms upstairs opening off a wide hall. The two bedrooms Mom and her brothers used to sleep in were filled with their old mahogany bedroom sets, the beds covered with white chenille spreads. A closet under the eaves in our uncles' old room held some of their toys: Big Little Books* and a metal toy car you could wind up and it would scoot around the room. We also found a wind-up playing card dealer *way* back in the closet, and we found out why Grandma put it there when we took it downstairs. If you wound it up really, really tight, it would hurl cards all over the living room, but . . . you had to pick up the cards if you wanted to do it again—which we did. Again and again and again.

In Mom's old room, the closet under the eaves was where Grandma stored Cashmere Bouquet soap, unwrapped, to dry it out "so it wouldn't get gummy in the soap dish."

The third room was Cile's bedroom, and her childhood dolls were displayed on a quilted cotton bedspread in a tiny print. A bright blue plaster piggy bank sat on the wide windowsill. The last room was Grandma's sewing room. Besides sewing all sorts of things, Grandma also embroidered, crocheted, and made

---

*Picture a comic book condensed into a very fat, roughly four-inch-square book with a hard cover. There was a separate little picture on the right-hand bottom corners that turned into a moving cartoon when you flipped through the pages.

baskets from very long pine needles she gathered in Florida.

At one side of the hall was a clothes chute. You could open the little door and toss in your dirty laundry, and the clothes would go all the way down two floors to the basement. There was a little door like that in the first-floor hallway, too. We used the laundry chute to send "secret messages" tied to a long string. (It was always hard to think of a secret message when we were already yelling to each other from floor to floor.)

Grandma's garden covered an entire city lot near her house, and she loved to work in it. Grandma and Cile worked together making pickles from her home-grown cucumbers, cooking raspberry and strawberry jam, canning yellow beans, green beans, tomatoes, and later, freezing vegetables and berries in milk cartons.

Around the garage, Grandma had planted tuberous begonias. In front of all the evergreens that lined the back and end of the triple-lot lawn at the side of their stone house were Grandma's peonies. She must have divided them, and divided them again and again, to fill all that space, because I can't picture Grandma lavishly spending money for that many peonies. I bet she took cuttings to make more begonias, too.

We loved being able to spend time with Grandma and Grandpa anytime we wanted.—*Susan*

Jean in front of Grandma's border of peonies and evergreens. (The red peonies on the right don't show up well in this circa-1957 black-and-white photo.)

How to Make More African Violets

Grandma Noffke really liked African violets and was good at growing them. She had quite a collection of beautiful violets in many colors to prove it. When Grandma and Grandpa Noffke went to Florida for the winter, Susie and I watered her violets, being careful to keep their leaves dry.

Grandma was very frugal, and to add more African violets to her collection she would often propagate them by simply cutting off a violet leaf with about a one-inch stem and pushing the stem into a pot of moist sand or soil. Miraculously, a new plant would develop from that one leaf. If one of Grandma's mature violet plants developed a "baby" plant next to it, Grandma would remove it from the parent plant with a sharp knife, making sure to keep its roots intact and plant it in a small pot.

Everybody says that I inherited Grandma Noffke's green thumb, but for some reason it doesn't seem to help me out when it comes to African violets; regretfully, I can't seem to keep them alive.—*Jean*

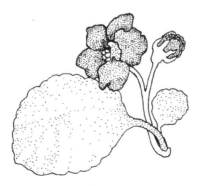

Diane: Aftermath of pin curl night
(Picture Day in second grade)

Home Permanents

Every girl wanted bouncy, curly hair in the fifties. Jean was born with it, but Diane and I needed some help. (Straight hair would be in style by the time our straight-haired little sister, Julie, came along.)

Pin curls were the usual solution. Mom twisted our just-washed, sopping-wet hair into organized rows of little coils, flattened and held by bobby pins. This was a normal Saturday routine, because Mom wanted us to look good for church on Sunday. (We can tell exactly which family photos were taken on a Saturday—Diane and I look like our heads have been slicked with Wildroot Cream Oil and our bobby pins are sticking out; Jean looks great.) The pin curls stayed in all of Saturday while we played, and our hair stayed wet for a long time all coiled up like that. We slept in those pin curls, too. I had slightly wavy hair to start with, so the resulting curls were very "boingy" and lasted for a while. Diane's hair was very straight, and with the first waft of humidity, her new curls were gone.

We saw Toni home permanents advertised on TV, and Mom bought a version for kids called Tonette. It was like having a beauty parlor in your own kitchen, and it smelled like one, too. We sat in chairs with towels over our shoulders while Mom used the plastic curlers and little papers from the box to wind our hair up tight. The next step was drenching our curler-covered hair with a horrible solution that smelled like ammonia. We had to hold big towels over our eyes to protect them from the noxious drips.

To make up for the misery of this process, Tonette boxes contained a toy of

How to Get Bouncy Fifties Hair with Pin Curls

We're leaving out the part about having your *mother* wash your hair—as you hang your head over the bathroom sink (or kneel next to the bathtub faucet) with a towel over your eyes and the pink rubber hose of the spray nozzle bobbing all over your neck . . .

You'll need bobby pins and a comb—the skinny tapered kind like barbers use works best.

1. Wash your hair and wrap it in a terry cloth bath towel, like a big turban, for about ten minutes to soak up some of the moisture (so *you* won't have to wait twenty-four hours for your pin curls to dry).

2. Comb out every snarl in your damp hair, and make a very straight part (an important part of good grooming in the pin curl era).

3. Starting at the top, by your face, use your comb to separate out about an inch-square section of hair and comb it smooth.

4. Using your pointer finger to hold down the base of the strand, wind the rest of the strand around that finger with your other hand (no twisting), making a coil and tucking the end part inside. Slip a bobby pin over both sides of the coil to hold it tight to your head. (You could use two bobby pins in an X—more secure for sleeping—but your curls will be double-dented.)

Continued on next page

5. Make a neat row of pin curls around the top of your head; then move down to make parallel rows of pin curls with the rest of your hair.

6. When your pin curls feel *completely* dry, you can take out the bobby pins and brush out your bouncy curls.

As little girls we never covered up our pin curls, but a grown-up lady would cover her pin curls with a headscarf made into a tropical-island-style turban: the headscarf folded into a triangle with the fold resting on the neck. The two side points were brought forward to the forehead and tied into a knot, and the middle point was brought forward and tucked *under* the knot. All the floppy ends were tucked in. (You might be able to carry a tray of bananas on your head.)

As a bigger girl, I read an article about looking beautiful at breakfast in a *Family Circle* or *Woman's Day* magazine that Mom brought home from the grocery store. The article featured photos of the actress Dina Merrill, a fine-boned tawny blonde serenely smiling while wearing orange lipstick and a silky orange robe at the breakfast table. (Was she also sipping *orange* juice?) Dina Merrill's hair was still in pin curls—but only bobby-pinned on one side of the coil, and the shiny blonde bumps on her elegant head hid the bobby pins. You might want to try that. I did.
—*Susan*

some sort to cut out. I don't remember what it was, and Diane doesn't either, but I bet Jean would know . . . because she never got one.*

After your hair was dry, the curlers were pulled out, but your hair stayed all coiled up. When you brushed it, it sprang right back and even if your hair was pretty long, your ears were going to show—for sure.

It was great not having to sleep in pin curls, but every time your hair got wet, you would notice that terrible ammonia smell, and as your hair grew, only the bottom part was curly. We didn't do this very often: pin curls weren't that bad after all.—*Susan*

* *I asked Jean, and she does remember what the toy was. There were paper dolls on the package that you could cut out—but only if you didn't already have naturally curly hair.*

Oom-pah-pah, Oom-pah-pah

"Susie should be taking music lessons and we don't have room for a piano.** How about the [fill in the un-coolest musical instrument you can think of]?"

At the age of nine I was sent to Ostwald's Academy of Music to master the accordion. There were accordions of many colors and sizes everywhere—no other instruments. I lasted a year.

Playing the accordion is like playing three musical instruments at the same time, or patting your head, rubbing your stomach . . . and jumping. Your left hand is pushing buttons, your right hand is playing the piano, and you are pulling the wretched thing in and out.

** *Until Uncle Keith gives us a piano!*

A "dress rehearsal" for one of our neighborhood shows. That's me at the left, and my costume seems to be the root beer–colored behemoth accordion. My friend Patsy is at the right, her sister, Mary Lou, is in front, and Diane and Jean are in the back.

My teacher, Beverly Rowe, a kind and patient lady, started me on a cute little accordion with twelve buttons and a short keyboard. I could have stopped there. I soon graduated to a root beer–colored behemoth that my scrawny arms could barely lift. The case, however, was an endless source of entertainment for me and my sisters. It was lined with velvet, and we spent more time drawing pictures with our fingers in the plushy velvet than I spent practicing.

Grandma Sanvidge, a rabid fan of *The Lawrence Welk Show*, kept saying I was going to be just like Myron Floren, who played the accordion on the show. Myron Floren was forty if he was a day, with crinkly light hair and a genial "I am having so much fun!" smile on his face the whole time he played. I was a nine-year-old girl, and I didn't want to be like Myron Floren.

Two things came out of this, one good, one bad:

1. Good: I did learn to read notes.

2. Bad: It took me a long time to "develop." I blame the big bad accordion and its nasty bellows for "nipping them in the bud." —*Susan*

St. Mary's Grade School

St. Mary's Grade School has been on the corner of Merritt Avenue and Boyd Street for a long time. We went to school there, and so did our mother. It is entirely surrounded by blacktop playground. A statue of Mary with outstretched arms overlooks a murky pond with goldfish. We saw Mary and the fish every day at recess.

St. Mary's Grade School, with the church in the background

There was a serious shortage of swings on that playground. Every swing was occupied and had a line of kids behind it waiting to get on. You could be a good sport and give the swinger a run-under, but then she might never get off.

You could jump rope—no waiting there. Our jump ropes were clothesline rope. You wrapped the end around your hands to get the right length and started jumping.

"Minnie, Minnie ha-ha.

Went to see her Pa-pa . . ."

Finish the rhyme with "Red hot peppers . . . 1, 2, 3, 4, 5 . . ."

Tag was another option. Everyone put a foot in, and the "Eeenie, Meenie, Minie, Mo" method determined who was "It." This was more popular with the boys, who didn't mind getting sweaty.

The older girls were too cool for games. They predicted their future with paper fortune tellers they had made and sneaked peeks at the cutest boys: "There's Kenny. I think he likes me."

One time Little Davie from Davie's Snack Bar drove onto the playground at the end of school in the Oscar Meyer Wienermobile. Neato!

Before school, we could play outside until the bell rang at 7:20 a.m. Then we lined up—no talking, no pushing—to go to church. We went to 7:30 Mass every single day. When you are Catholic you have to attend Mass once a week. Some math whizzes in my class calculated that after eighth-grade graduation we would not have to attend Mass again until we were forty-one years old.

Church over, we walked back across the playground into the school, past exposed pipes and radiators, across dark terrazzo floors, and into the cloak room to hang up our (cloaks?) coats and school bags. The smell of Murphy's Oil Soap brings this all back.

Our classroom was sunny with tall windows and big enough to hold thirty-five to forty-five students. It had a blackboard across the front with the Palmer Method of handwriting displayed above and a bookcase filled mostly with stories of the saints across the back. On top of the bookcase were a few straggly plants, a pencil sharpener, and a few pamphlets about the dangers of impure thoughts. White fingerprints left by eraser-clapping volunteers were on the door.

Some teachers arranged the students according to reading ability. The Brownies, the best readers, sat on the left, and the Elves, slow readers, on the right. Other teachers just tried to keep the talkers away from each other.

The bathroom for the lower-grade girls was just off the landing on the stairway to the second floor. It had a low ceiling, three kid-size sinks, and three stalls with kid-size toilets with black seats. Mr. Zuelke with his bucket of pink sawdust took care of mishaps.

Most of the teachers were nuns. Their habits caused constant speculation. Does Sister Giles have hair? How old *is* Sister Gerard? Shouldn't Sister DeChantal marry Father DuCharme?

We also had a few lay teachers, all women. My favorite was Mrs. Pfaffenroth, the second-grade teacher. We learned to read, said our First Confession, and made our First Communion that year.

The gym had a shiny wood floor, a balcony, and a stage with royal blue curtains. A circle with "SMS" in it was painted on the floor. The gym was used for basketball games (we watched from the balcony), Christmas programs, and the Fall Festival, and a couple of times they showed movies there: *Francis the Talking Mule* and *Rebecca of Sunnybrook Farm*.

There was a library upstairs for the older students and a bowling alley in the basement. The all-purpose room was used for recess in the winter, Camp Fire Girls and Cub Scout meetings, and the annual "Mother-Daughter Breakfast" and "Father-Daughter Dinner." (Didn't the boys ever get to do anything fun with their parents?)

The clock on the wall by the door says 3:15, and I hear the bell. We need to catch the bus. Where's my nickel?—*Diane*

Sign My Autograph Book, Please

For my birthday party in third grade I got a blue autograph book with a ponytailed girl on the front. I couldn't wait to fill up the pastel pages.

Continued on next page

Personal information first:
Name: Diane Sanvidge
School: St. Mary's
Club: Little Women 4-H Club
Favorite teacher: Mrs. Pfaffenroth
Best friend: Terry Compton
Boyfriend: ???
Movie: *Titanic* [1953 version]
Movie Star: Troy [Donahue]

Mom was the first to sign. She wrote:
Dear Diane,
Number two daughter
But not in my heart.
Sincerely, [!]
Mother [!]

Susan signed on a pink page with:
When you get married and live in a tree,
Send me down a coconut
C. (are)
O. (n)
D. (elivery)
Susie

Jean wrote on green:
B♯ [sharp]
Don't B♭ [flat]
Always B♮ [natural]
God bless you my sister
Jean Sanvidge

    I took the book to school. The teachers signed: "God bless you and love you always." "Love God and you will always be happy." "Good Luck, Diane."
    There were lots of "Roses are red, violets are blue" poems from my friends:
Roses are red. Violets are black.
Do me a favor and sit on a tack.

Roses are red. Violets are blue.
Skunks smell good compared to you.

Roses are wilted. Violets are dead.
Sugar is lumpy just like your head.

Continued on next page

Patsy Lux crammed two sentiments on her pink page:
In jail they give you coffee.
In jail they give you tea.
In jail they give you everything
Except the doggone key.

U R 2 good 2 B 4 gotten.

I took the book with me to Camp Hiwela and got
autographs from other campers:
I live in the city.
I live in the town.
I am the girl
Who spoiled your book
By writing upside down.

When you get married
And live by the lake
Send me a piece of
Your wedding cake.

I still have this little book and can remember every
person who signed it.—*Diane*

How to Make a Chinese Jump Rope . . .

. . . but (alas) not how to use it.

We made Chinese jump ropes by saving all the green rubber bands the paperboy used when he rolled up the newspapers. We looped them together one by one and tied the ends together.

Playing with a Chinese jump rope involved two girls stepping inside the big rubber band ring, stretching it into a big oblong with their ankles, and a third girl using a lot of fancy footwork with the parallel rubbery bands (like how your tongue plays with gum, but with your feet). Jean was the only one of us who was any good at this, and she remembers . . . that she was good at it.—*Susan*

1. Slip one rubber band inside another. Bring the left side of the rubber band up and over both sides of the other rubber band, pushing it down through its own right side.

2. As you pull the rubber bands tight, make sure it looks like this.

3. Continue making your Chinese jump rope by repeating the steps with the open rubber bands on either side. When your rubber band chain is long enough to make an oblong that will stretch to fit a girl (usually!) on each end and a jumper in the middle, tie the ends together with several tight knots to make sure it holds.

Jump Rope Rhymes We Have Known

The first one has haunted me for years. What is *that* all about?—*Susan*

Minnie Minnie Ha-ha
Went to see her pa-pa
Pa-pa dy-ing; Min-nie cry-ing
Minnie got a brand-new ba-by
Put it in the bathtub
See if it could swim
Drank up all the water
Ate a bar of soap
Tried to eat the bathtub
Wouldn't go down his throat
Along came the doctor
Along came the nurse
Along came the lady
With the alligator purse
Out went the doctor
Out went the nurse
Out went the lady
With the alligator purse.

I'm a little Dutch girl
Dressed in blue
These are the things
I like to do
Salute to the captain
Bow to the queen
Turn around
Like a submarine.
I can do a tap dance
I can do the splits
I can do the Hula
Just like this.

Teddy bear, teddy bear, dressed in blue,
Can you do what I tell you to?
Teddy bear, teddy bear, turn around.
Teddy bear, teddy bear, touch the ground.
Teddy bear, teddy bear, show your shoe.
Teddy bear, teddy bear, that will do.
Teddy bear, teddy bear, climb the stairs.
Teddy bear, teddy bear, say your prayers.
Teddy bear, teddy bear, turn out the light.
Teddy bear, teddy bear, say good night.

How to Make a Folded Paper Fortune Teller

You will need: an 8½-by-11-inch sheet of white paper and some crayons.

VALLEY FOLD ————————————

MOUNTAIN FOLD ·····························

1. Fold top left corner of paper down to meet right edge.

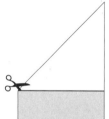

2. Cut off the excess paper so you have a large triangle.

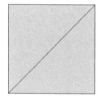

3. Open the triangle into a square. You have a diagonal "valley" fold.

4. Fold diagonally in the opposite direction to make another valley fold. Open it up.

5. Fold in each corner to the center to make more valley folds.

6. Make sure all the triangles are flattened down, and . . .

7. . . . flip it over. (You'll see "mountain" folds.)

8. Fold each corner in to the center.

9. Flip it over, and it looks like this.

10. Make a backward (mountain) fold on the vertical line separating the right and left squares. Open it up and . . .

11. . . . make a backward (mountain) fold on the horizontal center line. (You'll have a rectangle with a mountain fold on top.)

12. Hold the folded rectangle with both hands and press in and up to make a peak.

13. Pull out each loose triangle and fold out to make four "bird beaks," places for your fingers to work the fortune teller like a hand puppet.

14. The finished fortune teller is ready to color.

Continued on next page

How to Use the Fortune Teller

1. Color the outer faces of the fortune teller triangles red, yellow, blue, and green.

2. Number the inside triangles 1, 2, 3, 4, 5, 6, 7, and 8.

3. Write eight fortunes on the insides of the numbered flaps. For example:
   You will marry Richard.
   You will have 4 babies. (Of course you will, you're Catholic.)
   You will be famous when you grow up.
   You will find a lot of money and be rich.
   You will miss the bus. Wah!
   You will flunk arithmetic.
   You will lose your library book.
   You will be late for school.

4. Fold the fortune teller back to its finished shape. Hold the fortune teller so that your pointer fingers and thumbs are each inside a beak and that all the beak tips are together.

5. Say to your friend, "Pick a color."

6. As you spell out the name of the color your friend chooses, open and close the fortune teller as you say each letter, ending with the fortune teller open and numbers showing. For example:

   "R": Move the beaks in your left hand away from the beaks in your right hand. Move the beaks back together.

   "E": Move the beaks on your pointer fingers away from the beaks on your thumbs. Move the beaks back together.

   "D": Move the beaks in your left hand away from the beaks in your right hand. Hold that position.

7. Four numbers are showing. Say, "Pick a number."

8. As you count out the number your friend chooses, open and close the fortune teller. For example:

   "1": Move the beaks back together and then move the beaks on your pointer fingers apart from the beaks on your thumbs. Move the beaks back together.

   "2": Move the beaks in your left hand away from the beaks in your right hand. Move the beaks back together.

   "3": Move the beaks on your pointer fingers away from the beaks on your thumbs. Hold that position.

9. Again, four numbers are showing. Say, "Pick a number."

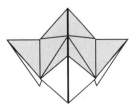

10. Lift the flap of the number your friend chooses and read the fortune underneath.

Polio

When we were in grade school, polio was a scary disease that was infecting kids our age. You could die from it, or if you lived, you might not be able to walk. We saw posters of kids in leg braces with crutches and pictures of kids with their tiny heads sticking out from the big Iron Lung that helped their paralyzed lungs breathe.

We collected dimes and put them in the cardboard folder from the March of Dimes that we got at school. We turned it in when it was full—five dollars' worth of dimes.

We watched the March of Dimes telethon on Channel 2. The poster child for the year was interviewed and always won our hearts. Other children, some with braces and some in wheelchairs, were brought out and the song was played: "Look at us we're walking. Look at us we're talking. We who never walked or talked before."

Local talent introduced by Colonel Caboose (Russ Widoe), our favorite kid's morning-show host, rounded out the program. Who wouldn't call in a pledge?

Susan remembers standing in line at school to get a polio shot. The vaccination program was discontinued before the rest of us got to school. In 1964, the oral polio vaccine was made available to all. Our whole family went to Webster Stanley School, where we stood in line to get a little paper cup holding a sugar cube that had the vaccine in it. We had to go three times, with a month between. Each dose was formulated for a different strain of the polio virus. The strains were simply named Type I, Type II, and Type III.—*Diane*

Here is my card:

IMMUNIZATION CERTIFICATE

You have received Sabin Oral Polio Vaccine.

Type I ☐   Type III ☐   Type II ☐
Date 3/15/64   Date APR 19 1964   Date 1964

IMPORTANT — Please keep this card and BRING IT WITH YOU WHEN YOU COME FOR YOUR NEXT DOSE OF POLIO VACCINE. Your physician will be notified of your immunizations.

Your Name   Diane Sanvidge

REMEMBER — You are not fully protected until you have had all three types of vaccine. Additional programs are scheduled for:

April 19 — Type III
May 17 — Type II

Best Friends

Patsy and her sister, Mary Lou, grew up in a house a half-block away from ours, and we were in and out of each other's houses so much the whole time we were growing up that they are like two more sisters.

Patricia Elaine Marie Catherine Lux has been my friend longer than anybody else: since we were three. Patsy is only five months older than me (Susan Marie Catherine Sanvidge), but always a year ahead of me in the same grade school, high school, and college. (We both chose Catherine as our Confirmation name.) She was (and is) talented, funny, smart, and neat.

Starting when she was very little, Patsy went to dance lessons, beginning with little-girl ballet and on to tap dancing. Every year her dance school had a recital, and Patsy had a closet full of costumes (in a variety of sizes)—satin, taffeta, sequins, sparkles, feathers, ruffles, ribbons—with funny little matching hats. She had soft pink ballet shoes and heavy shiny-black tap shoes in many sizes, too. One day Patsy let us all try on her costumes and taught us dance steps. It wasn't long before she had made up dance routines for the five of us. The

Susie is on the left and Patsy is on the right.

From left: Patsy, Mary Lou, Susie, Jean, and Diane, on our back stoop—all wearing Patsy's dance costumes

next step, of course, was to sell tickets in the neighborhood. We set up folding chairs on the oil-stained cement of the Luxes' garage, lifted the swing-up door, and had our first "Circus."

Many summers after that, when the days started feeling long, Patsy would teach us new dance routines, and we'd have another show. Each year more of the neighbor kids were in it, too. They couldn't all be in Patsy costumes, so our "Circus" became more like a real circus. At one of the shows, our friend Tommy made a stage curtain in our garage with a clothesline and an army blanket, and someone (was it Patsy?) convinced Tommy's older-than-us brother, Dickie, to sing "My Rubber Dolly," holding a rubber doll. It was a memorable performance—not one of us has forgotten it (except maybe grown-up Richard).

Patsy and I have spent hours and hours together, and we were always an effortless combination. "Patsy, do you want to come over and pick scabs?" "I'll be right over, Susie!" And then we'd sit on the back stoop for a leisurely pick at our itched-to-a-scab mosquito bites. We liked to do the same things. We spent days making our own paper dolls, coloring neatly within the lines of our coloring books—shading, outlining, trying colors on top of each other—and sewing "dream wardrobes" for our dolls. We plucked at our Mickey Mouse guitars (with P and S scrawled in silver on Mickey's ears, to tell them apart). Neither of us made what you could call music, but we did both like to dance. We were, and are, both Picky Eaters (frog legs, yuck!), so that wasn't different either.

But . . . Patsy could do cartwheels and stand on her head (I never could), and her precisely looped penmanship was way closer to the Palmer Method than mine. She used to scrape the toes of shoes she hated on the cement so she could get new ones; I would never have dared to do that.

As we grew up, both of us were art majors, library employees, and graphic designers, and we even held the same job a year apart. And when we get together now, being with Patsy *still* feels as comfortable as being with myself.—*Susan*

And now Jean is going to tell you about her friend Mary Lou.

Both Mom and Dad liked our friends Patsy and Mary Lou, and they affectionately referred to Mary Lou as Mary Lou-ou-ou. (Everybody had a nickname back then, didn't they? Mine was "Neenie" to all the littler kids in the neighborhood who couldn't say "Jeanie.")

Picture a girl version of Mutt and Jeff. Although Mary Lou's birthday and mine were only twenty-four days apart, we were an unlikely looking duo. She was petite and cute, and I was half a head taller and more than a few pounds heavier.

Mary Lou was always up for whatever play activity I'd suggest: riding our tricycles (later two-wheeler bikes), jumping rope, roller skating, hula hooping, playing house (I always had the dubious honor of being "the dad" since I was bigger), playing school, swinging on our swing set, playing with our Barbie dolls, hop-scotching, watching Shirley Temple movies (crying our eyes out), or just talking on the phone. (When she called, Dad would remind Mary Lou that we had just seen each other and it would cost her a quarter to talk to me.) Whatever we did, Mary Lou was always ready, willing, and able.

Oshkosh Northwestern

Our friendship even made the front page of the *Oshkosh Daily Northwestern.* The picture was taken when our kindergarten class took a field trip to the fire department. I'm standing in front, and that's Mary Lou behind me, sitting next to the fireman.

We had lots of options to choose from. If it was a nice summer day we could get out our hula hoops, clamp on our roller skates (if we could find the darn key), or practice walking on those stilts that Dad made for us. (I'm sure Susie or Diane won't mind if you use theirs, Mary Lou—they're not very good on them anyway.) If we got tired of those things, we could play paddle ball (try to get away with that one in the house!) or make bubbles from our little bottles of soapy mix with those little wands. (Definitely for outside, since it made Mom's washed and waxed floors slippery!)

If it was too hot or cold to be outside, Mary Lou and I could play on the basement stairs with our metal Slinkys, or if Mom had a potato to spare, we could play with our Mr. Potato Head in our playroom. Or if we were in the mood for a game, there was always the Cootie game (not to be confused with *getting* cooties), Tiddly Winks, or Pick-up Sticks.

We played dress-up with Mom's old dresses. (Doll dresses make good hats!) Our favorite of all dress-up outfits was Mom's bridesmaid dress from Uncle Hank and Aunt Dorie's wedding and the crownless net hat that went with it. Clopping around in Mom's old high heels was fun, too. (Just don't try going up or down stairs in them!)

Or should we play dolls? When I feed Tiny Tears her bottle, she wets her diaper and cries "real tears," too. We had little stand-up suitcases complete with little hangers and drawers to hold all our dolls' clothes and their accessories (until the basement flooded and ruined them). We cut out paper dolls. *McCall's* magazine even included a Betsy McCall paper doll and her paper outfits to cut out and play with, if you were lucky enough to have your mom subscribe to that. There was also a three-dimensional Betsy McCall Doll. And we played with the metal doll house with its plastic figures and furniture. (Guess Dad was too busy building real houses to make us a wooden doll house.)

About three o'clock in the afternoon of our play days, we would coyly inquire of the mom whose house we were playing at, "What's for supper?" If we didn't like the answer, we suddenly had to go to the other's house, only a half block away, to get something we desperately needed to play with. Of course, when we got there, the question was, "What's for supper?" If we didn't like that answer either, we'd have to choose the lesser evil and ask that mom if our friend could

Watching a Shirley Temple movie at Patsy and Mary Lou's house

eat over. I think Mary Lou's mom, Ginny, was onto us when she told us "steak and onions" and it turned out to be LIVER and onions! Yuck!

On occasion, Mary Lou and I would visit her dad's business, Tony's DeLuxe Tavern, named for her grandpa, down on the corner of Bowen and Otter. (It's still there today.) Upon entering, there was the distinct odor of stale beer and cigarette smoke, with more than a hint of cigar smoke. Mary Lou's dad, Vic, always seemed to have a cigar going.

We felt like big girls when we got to sit on those high bar stools and chug down a glass of pop, being sure to take time to spin around on our stools at least once or twice. The bar was usually full of neighborhood regulars who were always very friendly to us.

Mary Lou and I still see each other, but now it's over our favorite stir-fry at the Delta Restaurant in Oshkosh on Sawyer Street (which used to be the old Mars Restaurant when Mary Lou and I were in school together at Lourdes). We still look like Mutt and Jeff, but who cares when you've got a friend like Mary Lou.—*Jean*

How to Play Hopscotch

If you have a good friend like Mary Lou or Patsy, a sidewalk, and some chalk, you can play a game of hopscotch. Find as much chalk as you can (that rough cement is going to really eat it up) and draw a hopscotch pattern like this on the concrete. (You might want to get permission to do this, so you don't have to scrub the sidewalk if it's not okay.) Next find a small stone about an inch across for a marker.

Here's how to play:

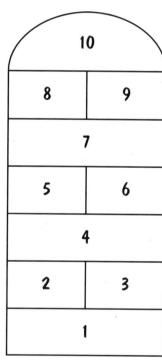

1. You can't step on any lines, and you'll be hopping square to square from one to ten and back. Hop into spaces 1, 4, 7, and 10 on one foot, and one-foot-in-each-square for 2/3, 5/6, 8/9. (One-two-one-two-one-two-one!)

2. The marker stone will be tossed into one square after another as you take turns—and you can't hop on a square with a marker in it.

3. Begin your turn by tossing your marker in space 1. Hop the grid, avoiding space 1. Land with one or both feet in 10, and jump to turn around. (The official rules will only let you hop with one foot on 10, but because I don't want you to fall over trying to spin around while hopping on one foot, *my* rules say it's okay to land with *two* feet on 10!)

4. Hop back through to 1, picking up your marker along the way and hopping out of the grid. And now it's your partner's turn to do the same thing.

5. Toss your marker in square 2 for the next turn, and do this for the rest of the number spaces, hopping through the grid each time.

6. Your turn is over if:
   —your marker lands in a wrong square when you toss it,
   —you step on a line or a space with a marker in it,
   —you lose your balance and fall over, or
   —you hop into a number space (other than 10!) with both feet.

The winner is the first player to successfully toss the marker on each successive number and hop all the way through the grid each time without breaking the rules. When in doubt about the rules, make up your own and all agree on it!

And remember, when you win, don't gloat. And if you lose, be a good sport about it and don't pout. Everybody hates braggers and poor sports!
—*Jean*

How to Write with Palmer Method Penmanship

We were taught to write with the loop-filled Palmer Method at St. Mary's Grade School. Some of these letters aren't *quite* the way I remember them. (For example, I know that Sister Gerard had us make big curls on the bottoms of our capital Ss in fifth grade, because writing my name uses two of them). When I tried out these letters, I remembered the finger bump we used to get in grade school from writing so much.

Find a few sheets of theme paper, sharpen a No. 2 pencil, and shake out your writing arm like Ed Norton did in *The Honeymooners* TV show. "Practice makes perfect!"—*Susan*

A B C D E F G H I
J K L M N O P Q R
S T U V W X Y Z

a b c d e f g h i
j k l m n o p q r
s t u v w x y z

The Legendary Cottage at Three Lakes

Grandma and Grandpa Noffke's cottage made a deep impression on all of us. When I developed allergies at age four, I spent an idyllic four months up there (just me) with Grandma, Grandpa, and Cile. All of the sisters spent time at the Three Lakes cottage without our parents. Our whole family went to Three Lakes at least once every summer, and every August we would go up with Mom for a week or more, while Dad and Grandpa were back in Oshkosh working. (Three Lakes is very far north in Wisconsin, close to Michigan's Upper Peninsula.)

There was never any whining about going to Grandma and Grandpa Noffke's cottage. We all liked being there. This was a very long time ago, but I can still remember what I saw out the car windows on the way there. (The first two hours of the trip was the route we took many, many times to our own cottage, but to get to Grandma and Grandpa's cottage we would drive farther north.) First we would see shabby resorts with little cabins. Soon there were swampy areas with dead trees sticking up out of the water, and then deep forests on both sides of the road. There were red signs by the side of the road. The signs would appear one after the other: "He lit a match," "to check gas tank," "that's why," "they call him," "skinless Frank." The last sign always said, "Burma Shave," and for a long time I didn't realize that these entertaining red signs, which were changed regularly, were an advertisement for shaving cream.

The straight road would get curvy and we'd see glimpses of lakes and signs for resorts. Then more and more fir trees appeared, and now the lakes were right by the side of the highway, and there were big signs for water ski shows. We were getting very close when we saw The Northernaire, a huge white fancy hotel and resort with coral red awnings and pennants flying from the roof, and Marty's Showboat, a restaurant that looked like a big ship.

The roads then began winding around lakes and more lakes. Signs advertising resorts, cottages, and boats were everywhere. Arrow signs—white boards with black letters spelling out the cottage owners' last names—were nailed one above the other on posts by the smaller roads. We couldn't wait to see the "Noffke" arrow pointing right.

There it is! We head down a smaller, winding road, past rough grass fields and sumacs. Cottages start appearing. As we drive on, the road gets narrower and the trees get taller. Soon there are only huge fir trees and the ground is totally covered with rust-colored, fragrant needles. The warm air smells like Christmas trees now, and we see Mrs. Telling's big swing set: we're very close! There's the Graves' house . . . and that's Grandma and Grandpa's cottage at the very end of the road, on a point with Laurel Lake on one side and Big Stone Lake on the other.

The lakes are sparkling through the trees. It's very quiet walking on the carpet of pine needles, and the air smells so good. We can hear distant motorboats.

On the "island" at Grandma and Grandpa Noffke's cottage on Big Stone Lake in Three Lakes, Wisconsin, from left to right, Jean, Susan, Mom, and Diane

Grandma and Cile are making us food in the big kitchen with the old wall-hung sink and a table that almost fills the rest of the room. Cupboards, with glass panes on top and solid wood doors below, cover one whole wall, and we see the little mugs we always use (butter yellow, robin's egg blue, tomato-soup red) through the glass. On the stove is a big pale green glass saltshaker with a dented aluminum top that has rice, or sometimes pieces of soda crackers, in it to keep the salt from clumping. (It was a little damp in the midst of all those evergreens.) Coffee is perking in a little enamel coffee pot on the stove. (The mornings were always cool at Grandma's cottage, which made coffee smell really good, even though I didn't drink coffee at the time.)

We can't wait to visit the "island." We walk a pine-needle-covered path through soft green grasses to a whitewashed bridge. Standing on the little bridge, we look for the water lilies in a shallow part of the lake on the left, and on the other side, it's the expanse of Big Stone Lake with boats and water skiers. And then we are on the "island," which has grass growing on it, and fieldstones around the edges to keep it from washing away. There are white Adirondack chairs to sit on, for fishing or just listening to the lake lapping all around.

In Grandma and Grandpa's cottage, there was knotty pine on all the walls and little cottage-y things like "A Fisherman's Prayer" hanging here and there. The living room was large but cozy, and the fieldstone fireplace had a bobcat pelt

The entire "island," with the whitewashed bridge at the right, water lilies in the foreground, and Big Stone Lake in the background

hanging on the wall over the pine mantelpiece. Grandma had made a dark wool braided rug big enough to cover the whole room. At one end of the living room was an old floor-model radio, which mainly produced static and squawks when Grandpa tried to tune in a baseball game. The windows, behind maple chairs with rough-striped cushions, looked out on a brushy woods with the lake twinkling through. Grandma had toys and games for us to play with in a big dark buffet with glass horse head bookends on it. (These were filled with pink and yellow cotton balls for some reason.) A deck of Old Maid cards and an Uncle Wiggily game were our favorite toys. Cile played these games with us and would often get to laughing so hard that tears would be streaming down her face.

At the very end of the living room was the front hall for a door that was only used to bring in the firewood stacked outside it. There was no real telephone in the cottage, except a *very* old-fashioned telephone—with a bell crank and a separate earpiece—hanging on the wall. It was only connected to the cottage of Grandma's friend Mrs. Telling, just on the other side of the point. Grandma would grind away at the bell crank and we'd hear her say, "Kew-hoo, Telling!" (She called her Telling.) Mrs. Telling was a cheerful, spunky, energetic lady who looked like a short, dark-haired Mary Martin. We liked her a lot. The Tellings rode horses, and they had a stable that we would walk past on the path to their very large, two-story cottage. Mrs. Telling's living room was

Diane and Susan on Mrs. Telling's beach. The little house behind us was for changing in and out of your swimming suit.

two stories high, open to the roof timbers, and the second-floor bedrooms opened off a balcony that overlooked the living room. Horse blankets and Indian blankets were hung on the balcony railing. Mrs. Telling had a beautiful sandy beach at her house, which we were welcome to use whenever we wanted to go swimming (and Grandma always made sure we didn't wear out that welcome).

Susan riding on the log carrier. You can see the huge hemlocks and the dappled sunlight in this picture.

Between the telephone and the fireplace in Grandma and Grandpa's living room was the door to Cile's bedroom. There was a large bay window in her room with little panes like French doors, and, in my memory, there is always a full moon out those windows. Once, Jean had to share a bed with Cile. The first night Jean was apparently thrashing all over the bed, and Cile brought this up many times all the next day. That night Jean had to sleep with Cile again, and she woke up completely stiff from keeping herself immobile all night.

Meanwhile, in a bedroom at the end of the hallway by the kitchen, Diane and I were sleeping comfortably in a big iron bed under a butter-yellow quilt with little red flowers. Grandma and Grandpa's bedroom was on the other end of the hallway, and the bathroom was in the middle. After Julie was born, the attic was remodeled to create another bedroom, and everybody was happy. The attic window above the bed faced the lake, and on sunny mornings the lake just shimmered and reflected all over the room.

There were more logs for the fireplace piled by the side of the garage (which had a white-washed, immaculately clean outhouse built into a back corner). A log carrier on wheels was our vehicle for giving each other rides, and we could walk to Mrs. Telling's big swing set by ourselves. The woods were not at all scary because you could see right through it everywhere. Very little grew through the thick blanket of fallen needles in the shade of those tall hemlocks (which is why it was a good place to go if you had allergies).

When we were up there in August, we always made an excursion to Rhinelander to buy school clothes, eat lunch in a restaurant, and order our favorite cream pies. Our visits to Rhinelander always seemed to coincide with Hodag Days. We had no idea what a hodag was back then, but that ugly creature was pictured everywhere. (I found out later that the hodag is a local legend: a dragonlike creature that is supposed to hold the spirits of hardworking, lumber-hauling oxen.)

Sometimes we went in to Three Lakes, where there were many places selling Indian souvenirs like little tomtoms, beaded purses, and moccasins. This is far north where it doesn't get that warm, and some stores sold warm woolen clothes even in summer.

I think of the meals we ate at Grandma and Grandpa's cottage as being real treats, but I don't know if this was more about being there and everything feeling so unrushed or how good the food always tasted up there. I do remember that Cile made the most delicious apple fritters, all hot and crunchy on the outside and soft, warm apple inside. And feasts of lobster tails with melted butter—to celebrate that we were there. We weren't the only ones enjoying ourselves at Grandma and Grandpa's cottage; all the grown-ups seemed relaxed, too.

This was a magic place. None of us will ever forget it.—*Susan*

Apple Fritters

Cile must have used the fritter batter recipe from *The Settlement Cook Book* (Grandma's only cookbook), because we have never found a written-down recipe. The *Settlement* specifies cutting the apples into round, cored slices and serving the fritters with powdered sugar and lemon, but Cile cut the apples in wedges and served the fritters with maple syrup. Fragrant, crispy-and-soft, delicious.—*Susan*

You will need: a heavy-duty pot or kettle for deep-frying and metal tongs to turn and retrieve the fritters. A deep-fry thermometer would be very helpful.

    1⅓ cups flour
    2 teaspoons baking powder
    ¼ teaspoon salt
    ⅔ cup milk (2% or whole milk, not skim milk)
    1 egg, well beaten
    2 tart apples (Granny Smith would be easiest to find now)
    vegetable oil for frying, 1½ inches deep in pot
    maple syrup

Continued on next page

From the Kitchen

Stir the flour, baking powder, and salt together. In a separate bowl, combine the milk and well-beaten egg. Make a well in the flour mixture and pour in milk/egg, mixing little by little from the center until combined into a very thick batter.

Pour 1½ inches of oil into the pot to heat up, keeping an eye on it as you prepare the apples. Heat the oil to 350° F (a 1-inch cube of bread will brown in 1 minute).

Peel the apples, cut in fourths, and remove cores. Cut each wedge into ⅓-inch slices. Gently mix the apples into the batter so they won't dry out while you wait for the oil to reach 350° F.

When the oil is hot, use tongs to retrieve (not-too-heavily-coated) apple slices one by one from the batter, and lower them into the hot oil. When one side is golden, flip to fry the other side. Make sure the oil temperature stays steady as you continue frying. (No sizzle: not hot enough. Dark brown: too hot.) Put cooked fritters on a platter covered with a few layers of paper towels for draining. (In the old days, the fritters would be draining on a paper bag.)

Serve warm with maple syrup.

The Late Fifties

Susie was ten, I had just turned eight, and Jean was almost seven, and this really neat thing happened: Julie was born just four days after my birthday. Get out the Teeter Babe and fold those diapers . . . Mom has three willing helpers.—*Diane*

"We're Getting a New Baby Sister!"

We knew exactly what day Julie would be born and told the nuns at St. Mary's that we would be getting a new baby sister on March 31. They smiled at us patronizingly and told us not to expect that. A Caesarean was scheduled for that day, and we all knew the baby would be a girl. We always had girls. Mom and Dad had a boy's name, Brian, ready for years—but never got to use it.

Julie was born right on schedule, and we were totally thrilled with our new

Mom holding a newborn Julie, with Jean and Diane (practicing with Jocko, a much-loved sock monkey) on the left, and Susan on the right

sister. We learned how to take care of her, and Mom never lacked willing babysitters. People kept saying to us, "The novelty will wear off," but it never did. We liked taking care of Julie, and we liked being able to teach her things.

I took charge of filling out her baby book. All three of us started watching Dr. Haim Ginott, a child psychologist on TV, and followed his advice. When it was time for the Tooth Fairy, I became Fairy Lucy and wrote tiny letters to leave under her pillow. (Julie figured this out when Fairy Lucy left her some gum and she saw me with the same brand.) When Julie was around eight, she started a little store in the basement called The Poppy Shoppe. We all thought this was really cute, and I even made her a little logo and receipts. As time went on, whenever we couldn't find something, we'd always ask: "Julie, did you sell it?" One time I went down in the basement and there, in Julie's Poppy Shoppe, were two big oil paintings I had done—a bargain at two dollars each (and still nobody bought them).

As Julie was growing up, she held her own with her older sisters. When I learned some French and Italian words, Julie was interested in learning them, too. When I was reading J. D. Salinger's *Franny and Zooey*, she wanted to read it, too. She listened to the same rock-and-roll music we did and took an interest

Diane taking care of little sister Julie at Boulder Lake

in our boyfriends, telling us who she liked and who she didn't. Julie and Diane shared a bedroom at the front of our house with a window right next to the front door. When we'd come home from dates, we would always hear a little scratching on the window screen at a well-chosen moment. There was Julie, wide awake, watching us. Once, when Jean was on the back porch for a while with her boyfriend, Julie tossed a little note out the door: "I do not want to be aunt!"

Around this time Julie noticed that Jean was always running out of money and offered to lend her some . . . with interest. This arrangement was quite profitable to Julie over the years.

Hey! We didn't think little baby sisters were supposed to be so smart!
—*Susan*

Julie Gets the Last Word

You girls had made me a whole wardrobe for first grade—a reversible jumper that went over a couple of shirtdresses, which could also be worn alone. Cute!

"Puh-ple!!! I hate puh-ple!"—Julie, age three (opening a present of purple slippers from Cile—while Cile was watching her)

Interestingly (no pun intended) enough, I charged Jean interest, but I hadn't advanced far enough in math to know how to calculate it. I'd say, "Let's see . . . ten dollars . . . three weeks . . . 4 percent interest . . . you owe me . . . uh . . . thirteen dollars," and she'd pay it! She did get me from time to time. I remember going "halvsies" on the 45 of "Hold Me, Thrill Me, Kiss Me" by Mel somebody. It cost me 50 cents, and she never let me touch it!—*Julie*

Meet the Neighbors: Our Bowen Street Neighborhood

We lived on the northeast side of Oshkosh across the street from Grandma Noffke. Our block had a nice mix of families, with and without kids, and new and old houses. Let's walk out the front door and take a walk around the block. We'll go south on Bowen Street first . . .

The Joneses live next door, where we used to live. Clifford Jones is tall, thin, and friendly. Carolyn is a great seamstress. She makes the most detailed doll clothes ever. Howie, their oldest child, is the owner of the most popular (and only) neighborhood wading pool. He fears getting "pounded in the ground" by our dad. One summer someone filled a little plastic lemon with water and squirted him in the stomach. There must have been leftover lemon juice in it because he didn't get tan in that spot for two years. Timmy is Julie's age, and Amy is the youngest. (She was so cute and nice that I named my first baby after her.)

Howie was very generous with his pool, or maybe he was just outnumbered? That's our 1956 "Two-Tone" Oldsmobile (red and white!) in the background.

An older couple live in the next house. They never yell at us, even though we are always cutting through their yard to get to the Schmidts' house.

The Schmidts live on the corner. Bill is a handsome weightlifter, an ex-navy man. Joanie has beautiful rosy skin, pitch-black shiny hair, and a big smile. She eats a Hershey's candy bar every day. Their toilet seat has a "Go Navy!" bumper sticker on it when you lift the lid, and there is a pile of knitting near every chair. Joanie makes sweaters for her kids with designs of puppies and kittens knit in Angora on the fronts. The Schmidt kids are Kathleen (who always said she was born on "September source"), Jeannie, Karen, Tom, Susie, and Heidi.

Dad always tells the story of Tommy Schmidt throwing clumps of mud on our driveway. "Tommy, did you throw this mud on my driveway?" "No." "Yes, you did. I saw you." "No, you didn't. You weren't home when I did it." BUSTED.

Turning the corner onto Nevada, there are two newer houses. The first one is the Hendricksons'. They have two daughters near our ages, but we've never really gotten to know them. Just around the corner on Evans Street is the Thompsons'. Peter and John play baseball with us. They have a little sister, Inga. One spring when, as usual, many of the backyards on the block were filled with water, Peter and John started out wading in, then started pushing each other in, and ended up just rolling around in the water, totally covered with mud. We watched the whole thing from our kitchen window.

The next house is an old but unfinished house, home to Mrs. Katie and her many cats. Mrs. Katie wears loose black dresses and has a long gray braid down her back. She uses our phone sometimes because she doesn't have one.

Next to Mrs. Katie's (and just behind our house) is the Krauses' little white house. Clarence "Butch" Krause is a vacuum cleaner salesman. Rosemary is a housewife (and sometimes a telephone operator who recognizes our voices). Denny, Bonnie, and Johnny are close in age to us, and we play with them a lot. In their backyard is a large garden and a water pump that almost took Johnny's finger off. (*Mom drove Johnny and his mother to the hospital.—Jean*)

Ruth, Wesley, and Sharon Dietrich live in the dark red house next door, which looks a lot like our cottage. They have an old two-story building at the back of their lot that they had to add a little bumped-out piece to so they could fit their new longer car in it. Ruth is very friendly and once called to wake us up when we overslept. Sharon is always very clean and dressed up. Wes was a nice, sort of shy man who died unexpectedly one summer. We all went to his funeral.

Next to the Dietrichs', a new house was built for the Reverend and Mrs. Gose. I don't remember seeing them except for trick-or-treating. One year the Reverend was sick and we had to walk back to his bedroom so he could see our costumes. I think that was the year I wore a paper bag over my head . . . a precursor to my Unknown Comic years?

Another new house was built just around the corner on Bent Avenue for the Hedings. Bob and DonnaBelle have three daughters. Bob is into trout fishing and works for the DNR. He and Dad get along great.

The next house, on the corner of Bent and Bowen Street (Patsy and

Mary Lou Lux live just across the street), is old and the home of the Hunkes. Ray Hunke spends a lot of time cutting wood with a chain saw. His wife, Lucille, is a sweet person. They have two sons.

There were two vacant lots between the Hunkes' and our house for a long time. We would dig for potatoes in the abandoned garden of one of them. (There was probably a house torn down there?) Eventually both lots had new houses on them. One house has a couple with no kids, and the other is our next-door neighbors, the Kuhns. Bob and Marlene have two sons, Rusty and David, who is

There won't be an empty lot next door anymore. The Kuhns will be our new neighbors. Diane and Jean are playing with Bonnie and Denny Krause on the dirt excavated from the Kuhns' future basement.

Julie's age. (*Later they had a little sister named Kim. Bob was a commercial artist who drew cartoon characters for Birds Eye Frozen Vegetables.—Jean*) Pretty soon new neighbors will move in, and the new neighbor lady will wear a two-piece swimming suit all summer long.

We're almost home now. Want an Alaska-Pop? We've got some in the freezer.—*Diane*

Christmas Trees We Have Known

Grandma Noffke, a practical woman with an uncluttered house, always had a big sprawling Christmas tree—nearly as wide as it was tall (like Grandpa). It was a real adventure to belly-crawl under the tree in our fluffy petticoats, stiff nylon Christmas dresses, and slippery patent leather shoes to find our presents. The lights on Grandma Noffke's tree were extra big with pointy tips and ridges, the kind you usually see on outside trees, and the tree branches looked almost yellow in all that bright, multicolored light. Grandma had long spiky glass ornaments, ornaments with decorative dents, see-through colored-glass balls with painted stripes, and strands of tinsel on her tree.

Grandma Sanvidge, queen of a knickknack kingdom, had Christmas trees that were small enough to put on a table. I don't remember a single ornament. Every year, her trees got smaller and smaller, until one year she didn't have a Christmas tree at all. Do I hear Mom saying, "That is so sad"?

Aunt Dorie, whose dishes and furniture were very modernistic, had Christmas trees to match. One year her long-needled pine tree was completely white with flocking and had all pink ornaments; another year she had an aluminum tree with revolving colored lights making the tree a different color every few minutes.

At our own house, Christmas trees were the short-needled kind, and always fragrant, but they were hardly ever what you might call "handsome specimens." Buying a Christmas tree was never a family excursion, and my suspicion is this: Dad was the one who picked them out, and it wasn't his favorite thing to do. I can picture Dad, after an entire day working in unheated houses or outside in the freezing cold, stopping by the freezing-cold Christmas tree lot—and buying the first tree he saw.

One of our Christmas trees will live in infamy. It was so bad that Mom and Dad's friend Romie told Mom he would take it down to his Pontiac dealership garage and put flocking on it. As Romie finished spraying the tree, he noticed Dad's truck at Kelley's Bakery across the street and took the tree over there. When Dad saw it, he said, "That tree is uglier than the one I got," and Romie answered, "This *is* your tree!" Del Kelley teased Dad about that tree for years. (Mom remembers that it was *aluminum paint* that Romie put on that tree, but the three older sisters think we would have whined so much about not being able to *smell* the Christmas tree, and having a *real* tree sprayed with car-bumper-aluminum paint, that we certainly would have remembered it.)

Our tree: The wire from the lights drops through at least a foot of nothingness to finally reach another branch. That year we each got a doll whose hair color matched our own. Grandma Noffke made flannel pajamas for us and matching pajamas for our new dolls.

Mom had to resort to flocking yet another Christmas tree. After we had all the ornaments on, it still looked bad, so she sprayed on even more flocking "to fill it out a little more." Ever since then, there have been little bits of flocking on all of our oldest ornaments.

It was always Dad who put the tree in the stand and did the lights (this part he liked; he was in a nice, warm living room), while we brought the ornament boxes down from the attic and put on Christmas music. Each of us searched for our favorites among the crumpled tissue wrappings, and my favorite ornament was a silver-and-blue star. We usually had tinsel ropes on the tree; strands of tinsel only a few times. We were never successful making popcorn chains—we liked to eat popcorn too much. One year, influenced by Aunt Dorie's modernistic

At Uncle Hank and Aunt Dorie's house, with Grandma Noffke. Our cousin Kathy (in front) is a little too young to know what's going on, but Diane and I are just lit up with Christmas spirit. Jean just remembered what she forgot to ask for in her letter to Santa.

pink-and-white tree, Mom bought all pink lights, pink glass ball ornaments, and pink tinsel rope. She only did that once—it just didn't feel Christmassy enough to any of us. (We had some of those leftover pink ornaments on the tree every year after that.)

After our tree was all decorated, we turned out every light in the room and let the Christmas tree lights and the scent of the warming branches make us feel all Christmassy. We had some fat little snowman candles that we always put on tables (and never burned), and there was a wreath on the front door, but there weren't as many Christmas decorations all over the house as people have now.

Having the Christmas tree decorated meant Christmas was coming soon. It was time to finish our Christmas shopping! Buying presents for five people is a real challenge when you earn only fifty cents a week. Kresge's in downtown Oshkosh was even cheaper than Woolworth's (both were "dime stores"), and Mom took us there to shop. A tiny plastic baby doll was a real deal at ten cents! (Wouldn't Mom just love one of these?) I'm pretty sure Jean was the lucky person who got a brand-new fifty-cent blouse that year. (It looked like a fifty-cent blouse.) Miniature plants, real fish, a kite, little pencils! If the price was right, it was going to be a present for somebody. We loved wrapping presents,

"Can we open just *one* present now?"
—Susan or Diane or Jean or Julie

rearranging the growing pile under the tree, and waking up to the intoxicating whiff of the Christmas tree.

One holiday season we had Santa Claus pins to wear on our winter coats. The squared-off Santa face had a tiny red bulb for a nose and a little string to pull and make the nose light up. We used the little red Santa noses to read under the covers when we were supposed to be sleeping. (Our parents must have known about this and feared eye problems because the next year we got kid-size flashlights.)

One year, we pooled our resources (supplemented with babysitting money by that time) and bought Dad a new pipe. Dad could shake a present once and guess what it was, so we decided to put the little box into a bigger box and that box into a bigger box, and that box . . . By the time we were done, the box we wrapped could have held a bushel basket. Every space was stuffed with newspaper. Dad shook it once (there was no sound at all) and said, "It's a pipe."

Christmas after Christmas passed with big family dinners, Christmas cookies, and Hughes' chocolates, and a while back, Mom gave us each our favorite ornaments to put on our own trees. The silver-and-blue star is at my house now. I'm afraid I'm taking after Grandma Sanvidge in the Christmas tree category. I did have tall, short-needled, and fragrant Christmas trees every year for a long time (not always handsome specimens), and I always put the old silver-and-blue star on the Christmas tree myself.—*Susan*

And here it is.

"Santa Looks a Lot Like . . ."

Maybe you've heard that popular song "Santa Looked a Lot Like Daddy"?

When my sisters and I were children, Dr. Louis D. Graber was our family doctor. He was also a former neighbor (from when Mom and Dad lived on Powers Street in Oshkosh), a family friend, and . . . Santa Claus.

On Christmas Eve, when we were at Aunt Dorie and Uncle Hank's house with our little cousins, Santa Claus would appear with a bag of presents. Dr. Graber was the perfect embodiment of the jolly old fellow. I don't even remember what he gave us, it was just that *he was there in person handing me a present!*

What amazes me, when I think back about it, is how a busy doctor

Uncle Hank, Aunt Dorie (with Chuckie), and Stevie meet Santa Claus (Dr. Graber) in person, at their own house.

with a large family of his own could take time out on Christmas Eve to don that special red suit and come to *our* Christmas gathering. We were thrilled at the very sight of him!

It was Susie who first noticed that Santa Claus looked a lot like Dr. Graber, and she mentioned it to Mom, who most likely told her at this point that her suspicions were correct, but "Don't spoil it for your sisters!"

I'm afraid I was a ripe old ten before becoming an unbeliever. I would refute my classmates with "But I saw him!" When I recognized him, I did say to Mom, "Santa Claus looks a lot like Dr. Graber." She just looked at me, and I said, "He is, isn't he?" and she said, "Don't spoil it for Julie." (Notice that she didn't say anything about Diane and Jean, who had probably wised up long before I did.)—Susan

In later years, I wrote to Dr. Graber and thanked him for his kindness and generosity. He wrote back and in his letter said, "Your father did me so many favors."

My husband and I know the joy and excitement that Santa brings as we ourselves don those special red outfits and portray the jolly couple every year.—*Jean*

Sauerkraut Candy

You could use pieces of Sauerkraut Candy as play-food sauerkraut with the set of little dishes you just got for Christmas, because it looks just like its namesake. It's actually shreds of coconut mixed in tawny sugary fudge (quite delicious)—but I always hesitated when I reached for a piece.

My friend Nooker's mother made Sauerkraut Candy every Christmas, and this is her recipe. (We couldn't find ours.) We added details to Vera Baier's brief recipe which Nooker had copied in the back of one of her mother's cookbooks long ago.—*Susan*

You will need: a candy thermometer

2 cups light brown sugar, packed
¾ cup milk (2% or whole, not skim milk)
2 tablespoons butter
1 teaspoon vanilla
2 cups grated coconut (Baker's Angel Flake)

Cook sugar and milk together in a pan over medium heat, stirring occasionally, until the candy thermometer reaches the "soft ball" stage (235° F). Stir in butter and remove from stove.

When lukewarm, stir in vanilla, then coconut. Beat to combine. When mixture has cooled enough to hold its shape on a spoon, drop onto wax paper in little heaps. Store in a tin between layers of wax paper.

Grandma Sanvidge

Grandma and Grandpa Sanvidge lived in a big old brick farmhouse south of Oshkosh. There was an old stone garage next to the road, an Oshkosh Cutting Die sign, and a parking lot of a driveway. Grandpa's shop was straight ahead of you when you pulled into the driveway. The huge lawn had a stone fence in the back where the property of the Miller Girls began.

A sidewalk led to the house, and you would go through an enclosed porch (that usually smelled like apples) to get to Grandma's kitchen. Her kitchen was huge. It had a table with fruit decals on the ends and a hanging bird cage, with parakeets in it, way back in the corner by a little window. There were bright little knickknacks everywhere. A brown cookie jar sat by the window. Inside, a plastic bag held dark brown refrigerator cookies that were crisp "just the way Grandpa liked them." I liked them, too.

This is Grandma Sanvidge (Ruth Safford Sanvidge) at our house, about to tell you what she bought at the "tea store." (That's what she called the A&P grocery store—which, we just found out, used to be called The Great Atlantic and Pacific *Tea* Company.) She also called frying pans "spiders," and attics were "garrets."

Grandma collected salt and pepper shakers and displayed them in a china cabinet with a curved glass front. We checked them out every time we visited. Our favorites were the toaster with little brown and ivory slices of "toast" that were the shakers, the pink ham in the black frying pan, the ladies' high heel shoes, and the bride and groom (turn them around to see what they would look like later). There were lots more collected on trips with names of places they had visited with their friends. The cabinet was taller than we were, and every shelf was filled with salt and pepper shakers all the way to the back.

Just off the kitchen, Grandma had the biggest bathroom. It was blue and yellow with a window at each end and had lots of thick, fluffy towels.

On the other side of the kitchen, by the salt and pepper shaker cabinet, was the doorway to the living room. The living room was wallpapered, with white woodwork and lots of knickknacks. A swiveling green-vinyl upholstered rocking chair sat in the bay window. Grandpa always sat there. A long couch (that had a plastic slipcover on it for a while) was on the west wall. We always sat there with Mom and Dad until Grandma brought out the toys: an odd selection featuring a battery-operated bartender!

There were four doors off the living room. Near the bay window alcove where Grandpa always sat was the entrance to a narrow enclosed front porch that we never went in. (Maybe because there was a scary cast-iron doorstop that looked like a big bug, holding the door open.) A lighted Santa face was always displayed in the window here at Christmastime. (For a while there was a big plywood snowman display in the yard, instead.)

Grandma and Grandpa's bedroom was through the next doorway. It was a big room with twin beds, but I don't remember much more about it, except that there were electric blankets on the beds and there was lots of green in the room.

Nearby was a door to a stairway that led to an apartment upstairs (with no bathroom). In the fifties and early sixties, Helen Nancy (our dad's cousin) and her husband lived there with their children. Later, after they had built their own house near Grandpa's shop, Grandma's widowed sister-in-law moved in with her little Pomeranian dog, Tiger.

The last door, near the kitchen, was the guest bedroom. This was where we slept when we stayed overnight at Grandma's. The room was small, but there were two big windows and a comfortable bed with ironed sheets, pillowcases embroidered by Grandma, and an electric blanket. There was a dressing table with a big mirror and a Mogen David wine bottle with change in it that Grandma always let us count. A picture of our oldest cousin Johnny as a baby with his mother (Aunt Lorraine) was on the wall above the bed.

Grandma got her hair done every Friday at 1:00 p.m. at LaVern's Beauty Shop just down the highway from her house. She wore powder on her smooth skin, red lipstick almost always, and red nail polish sometimes. She had a stylish wardrobe with suits and dresses, and a *mink stole*.

When she was cooking or cleaning, she wore over-the-head print aprons with bright piping on the edges and a big pocket at the bottom, and canvas shoes with soft soles. Grandma was a good cook. Creamed potatoes, pork chops, and her cookies are what I remember most, but everything was delicious. When you did the dishes with Grandma, she always washed. One of the parakeets in Grandma's kitchen was named Peetie. Once during dinner Grandma noticed it was dead and said, "Look, Vic, the parakeet is dead." And kept eating. When Grandma and Grandpa came up to our cottage, Grandma brought along an old Indian basket full of food she'd made, including her famous cookies. If Grandma was driving, they got there really fast.—*Diane*

Peaches and Cream

When the peaches were ripe in late summer, Grandma put on her apron, set a pot of water on to boil, and brought out her Blue Willow bowls.
—*Susan and Diane*

Fresh ripe peaches
1 tablespoon of sugar per peach
Cream

Put each peach in boiling water for about 3 minutes (to loosen the skin). Use a slotted spoon to lift the peaches from the water and peel off the skin. Slice the peeled peaches into a bowl and sprinkle on the tablespoon of sugar as you slice each one—to keep the peaches from browning and to bring out the juices.

Serve in a big bowl with a pitcher of cream on the side.

"Don't Sit Too Close to That Thing!"

Television was a new thing when we were kids. The screen was small and the picture was black-and-white, but we were enthralled. Sometimes we were so enthralled we would just stand there, in front of the screen, and Dad would holler: "Sit down! You make a better door than a window!"

I watched as much TV as I could get away with. It was the next best thing to playing outside. Watching Shirley Temple movies with Patsy and Mary Lou at their house was a favorite with all of us.

Jean wasn't quite two years old when we got our first television set. Our parents ordered it from a man they knew (his kids went to our school) who ran a business from his house selling new TVs and repairing them. Mom says the first thing we watched was Dwight D. Eisenhower's inauguration in January 1953. My earliest memory of our first TV is seeing a new piece of furniture in our living room up against the picture window drapes, right next to our front hall. I had just turned five and what I remember most about that first TV is sitting on the carpet in front of it—still in that odd location—staring at a test pattern. Technical difficulties, "snow," and an endlessly rolling picture were common in those early days of TV, and I can still picture Dave, in his repairman role, pulling out big glass tubes from the back of the TV and laying them on the carpet.—Susan

These were our favorite shows:

- *Ding Dong School*: Miss Frances made me feel like I was right there with her as she rang her Ding Dong School bell. Susie, Diane, and I all learned from Miss Frances. By the time Julie was watching TV, this show was off the air.

- *Captain Kangaroo*: He got that name from the big pockets (like a kangaroo's pouch) in the train conductor–type jacket he wore. His pockets were stuffed with toys or carrots. Some of Captain Kangaroo's companions were Mr. Green Jeans, Bunny Rabbit (the carrots were for him), Dancing Bear, the Banana Man, and Grandfather Clock.

The Howdy Doody Show: With Buffalo Bob, Clarabelle the Clown, Heidi Doody (Howdy's sister), Major Phineas T. Bluster, Dilly Dally, Princess Summerfall Winterspring, and Flub-a-Dub. We loved singing along to their theme song—"It's Howdy Doody time, it's Howdy Doody time"—and we imagined we were in the peanut gallery (where kids visiting the show would sit).

Colonel Caboose: A local show with Russ Widoe as the Colonel and his dodo bird companion. We saw cartoons on this show and were often tempted by pets to adopt from the local animal shelter. Where we grew up, Colonel Caboose was even more famous than Captain Kangaroo.

Kukla, Fran and Ollie: Fran was a lady. Ollie was a puppet who looked sort of like a dragon with a big snaggle tooth. Kukla was a puppet, too, and I don't know what he was supposed to be.

The Cisco Kid: With his sidekick, Pancho: "Hey, Cisco, wait for me!"

The Roy Rogers Show: Also starring Roy's pretty wife, Dale Evans. "Happy trails to you, until we meet again . . ."

The Lone Ranger: With his faithful companion, Tonto. "Heigh-ho, Silver!" (Silver was his horse.) The Lone Ranger always sounded like his sinuses were plugged up.

- *Sky King*: He was a pilot with a cheerful niece, Penny. He also sounded like his sinuses were plugged.

- *Winky Dink and You*: You had to order a magic green sheet so you could write on the TV screen and not get yelled at (even though it meant you had to be too close for whatever bad stuff the TV emitted). Winky Dink would "need help," and you had to draw the bridge or whatever he needed.

Dad: "I turned that damn thing off!"
Us: "But Dad, Winky Dink needs our help!"
Grandma (to herself): "They can't really believe that??"

- *The Ed Sullivan Show*: A "really good 'shew'" featuring Topo Gigio (a mouse puppet) and a variety of other performers including Elvis Presley in his first-ever TV performance. Mom said he'd never make it.

- *The Lawrence Welk Show*: With Joanne Castle, Myron Floren, and the Lennon Sisters. "Ah-one and ah-two . . ."

- *Your Hit Parade*: The latest songs were performed. (*But the "hits" were not what you would call teen favorites.—Susan*)

- *Name That Tune*: We played a version of this game show in the car on the way to the cottage. Dad would whistle the songs for us, and we would try to guess the names.

- *The Three Stooges*: Curly, Larry, and Moe are still making people laugh.

Eating Chocolates Like Olive Oyl

We spent hours and hours watching Popeye cartoons. To this day, when I open a tin can and pull back the lid, I am picturing Popeye gulk-gulk-gulking down his can of spinach. When somebody thanks me, I have to resist a flourishing bow and a "Salami, salami, baloney!" Is that my friend I see over there? "Yoo-hoo, Princey!" (I am not the only one of my sisters to do this.)

In one of my favorite cartoons, Olive Oyl is sprawled on a chaise longue, all gangly arms and legs, feet like tongue depressors, with a box of chocolates at her side. Give me a box of chocolates (Hughes' creams, please), and I'll show you exactly how she eats them. A three-part extravagant "ga-lunk," like operating a rubbery backhoe, then into the mouth, whole: gu-u-ulp! I am compelled to demonstrate this at least once per box of chocolates.

Olive Oyl had a big influence on me. I looked in the mirror one day and realized I was dressed like her, too— turtleneck, long skirt, black boots, and my hair in a little bun ..."Oh, *Popeye!*"—*Susan*

I'm Flying Like Peter Pan

Peter Pan, with Mary Martin playing Peter, was on TV for the first time when I had just turned seven. My sisters and I loved every terrifying and exhilarating minute of this show. Peter Pan (we thought he was the same age as we were) never wanted to grow up, had amazing adventures—and he could *fly*. We believed what Peter told us: if you crowed like a rooster, "er-er-EROO!!!" and jumped off something high enough, you could actually fly! We were crowing and jumping off chairs for weeks after.

My son was about seven when I found out that the old version of *Peter Pan* was going to be on television again, and I told him how much I had loved this show when I was his age. We sat down on the couch to watch it, and I was shocked to see Peter Pan "flying" with the undisguised aid of huge cables. Then my son said, "Why is Peter Pan a lady?"—*Susan*

Postscript: Years later, in the days before a Big Birthday, I found myself humming the same song over and over again, and then realized what it was: "I Won't Grow Up" from Peter Pan.

■ *What's My Line?, You Bet Your Life, The $64,000 Question,* and *I've Got a Secret:* These were all game shows. We all enjoyed playing along and imagined how many Alaska-Pops we could buy if we won.

■ *The Donna Reed Show, Father Knows Best, Leave It to Beaver,* and *Ozzie and Harriet:* Such perfect families. Psychiatrists everywhere have made a lot of money because of these shows.

■ *Bonanza, Gunsmoke,* and *Wagon Train:* These were cowboy shows that Dad really enjoyed, if we weren't standing in front of the TV screen!

■ *Sing Along with Mitch:* The Mitch Miller singers would sing musty old standards, and the words were printed on the bottom of the screen: "Follow the bouncing ball and SING!" Believe it or not, we liked this. We sang. All of us.

■ *The Mickey Mouse Club:* We sent in for our mouse ears and wore them while we watched this show. We were official members. Annette, Bobbie, Karen, and Cubbie were among our favorite Mouseketeers. "Spin and Marty" was a great series on this show. "Corky and White Shadow" was another . . . "M-I-C (pause) K-E-Y (pause) M-O-U-S-E . . ."

■ Cartoons: *Popeye* with Olive Oyl, Bluto, and Wimpy ("I will gladly pay you Tuesday, for a hamburger today."); *Mighty Mouse* ("Here I come to save the day!"); the Disney cartoons with Mickey and Minnie Mouse, Donald Duck, Goofy, and Pluto; Woody Woodpecker, Heckle and Jeckle, Bugs Bunny, Elmer Fudd, Yosemite Sam, and Daffy Duck; *Quick Draw McGraw; Tom Terrific* (The Greatest Hero Ever); *Rocky and Bullwinkle* (with Boris

Badenov and Natasha); and last, but not least, *Dudley Do-right of the Canadian Mounties*, whose first name would become our name for a bra. Why? Because our first bras had rows of crudely stitched ballerinas and their craggy profiles looked just like Dudley's.—*Jean*

Somehow, we found time to play outside, too.—Susan

Opening Up Our Closet Doors—in the Fifties

Dad was a pretty safe bet clothing-wise. He worked in the same Oshkosh B'Gosh pants and overalls year after year and usually wore them with plain white

T-shirts. Dad had so many red plaid wool Pendleton shirts over the years that we think of him every time we see one. Dad avoided dressing up whenever possible, and when he was forced to, we were likely to hear him mutter, "A necktie might as well be a noose."

When she wasn't "using up" our old pedal-pushers, Mom was very much in style. (She went to millinery school and had her own hat shop before she married Dad.) Her going-out dresses in the fifties had fitted waists, very full or very straight skirts, and swoopy necklines. Her white-dashes-on-navy swirly coat with matching hat (in the photo here) delighted us when we later got to use it for dress-up. The

Who are these stylish people? Diane, Mom, and Dad!

lining was a gorgeous red taffeta and the coat was so much fun to swish around in like Loretta Young did with her voluminous skirts when she glided down the magnificent staircase on her TV show. Mom had a really beautiful celery green Easter suit with a boxy jacket and a straight skirt, and she bought a new hat to match: a "cloche," with loose white flowers on pale green. When the new pointy-toed shoes came out, Mom was the first of her friends to buy a pair.

Meanwhile, Diane, Jean, and I went from pretty Kate Greenaway dresses with gathered skirts and sturdy Buster Brown shoes with thin folded-over ankle socks, to poodle skirts, sweater sets, saddle shoes, and swivel-straps, the next best thing to big-girl "slip-ons." (You could wear the shoes as slip-ons by rotating the strap back.) When Mom was in the hospital having Julie, Dad bought the three of us complete Easter outfits, from head to toe. My first swivel-straps, my much-loved "Ruby Slippers," came from that shopping trip. They were raspberry red patent leather with brass cobweb decorations, and I felt like Dorothy in *The Wizard of Oz* in them. It was hard not to click my heels all the time. We had flower-sprigged hats, white gloves, and little purses. As summer approached, we were handed the Montgomery Ward catalog to choose our summer clothes, and Mom took us out to buy tennis shoes.

On one of the annual back-to-school shopping trips in Rhinelander (near Grandma Noffke's cottage), I got my first "little black dress." I was eight, and I called it my Mambo Dress. It had lemon yellow piping and orange and yellow flowers on a black background, and a new feature that year: it was "low-waisted."

We had the warmest, best-made, fuzzy winter coats. They were made of heavy wool and always came with bulky matching snow pants and matching hats. One year, I chose a dark green twill (unfuzzy) "storm coat" with an odd fur-trimmed hat that looked like it belonged on a boy (one who wanted to be an airplane pilot when he grew up). I looked like I was in training for the WACs.

Every Christmas, we would each get to pick out a special Christmas dress at

The Lullabye Shoppe or at Toys and Togs. In seventh grade (officially a teenager), I was a girl's size 12, and my clothes were *still* coming from The Lullabye Shoppe and Toys and Togs. One day a classmate asked the dreaded question: Where did you get your dress? I knew *exactly* where (Toys and Togs!) I got my (Toys and Togs!) dress. After briefly considering eternal damnation, I answered, "I forgot." The dresses *were* interesting and pretty, even if they were from stores with really embarrassing names.

Pretty soon Julie would be the only sister wearing dresses from Toys and Togs. —*Susan*

Start a Fad!

A totally out-of-style "hand-me-down," an oddball gift, clothes that didn't fit at all or were obviously way too practical . . . I remember trying these things on, looking grimly into the mirror—and hearing Mom chirp, "Start a fad!" We didn't think we could start a fad (for thick, flesh-colored tights with fuzzballs? "Dutchy" frumpy dresses?), but *following* fads was another story. That, we did.

Conservative, sensible fads:

Circle pins on plain little blouses with Peter Pan collars. This much sought-after pin was a plain round silver circle. You pinned the ends of your already-prim, tight little collar together with it. (Peter Pan collars were round, flat collars.) Add the plainest of Orlon cardigans, and presto!—you look like you get all A's.

Creamy-white Wigwam wool socks and penny loafers. A fall and winter fad. Warm, thick Wigwam socks were not quite midcalf high—the rest of your leg

Diane, mugging for the camera (with Jean, Julie, and Kathy Schmidt), is wearing a red-and-white "skort." It's a skirt! It's shorts! (The shorts part was underneath, with elastic around the bottom of the legs.)

would freeze while you waited for the bus, but your toes would be toasty. I don't know who first had the idea of putting a penny in the odd little opening across the front of these hard-soled leather shoes. (People are still wearing penny loafers, so maybe it's no longer a fad?) If you had two and a half friends wearing fully loaded penny loafers, they could help you out if you lost your bus money. Rebellious types put dimes in their penny loafers. (They *always* had bus money—for four.)

Less conservative:

Tiny, square silk scarves. Fold it into a triangle and tie this tiny, tiny scarf under your chin with a tiny little knot. If you inherited Grandpa Noffke's big head, the scarf will be so tight that you will see the outline of your ears. Make sure the color of the scarf matches one of the colors in your print dress or skirt—the color you can barely see.

Poodle skirts. Who would think that an appliquéd poodle on a felt circle skirt (lay it flat and it makes a circle) with three-dimensional trimmed-poodle puffs, a red tongue, button eyes, and a string leash would be something every girl would really, really want? We had *multiple* poodle skirts.

Masses of fluffy petticoats. Your poodle skirt (or any other full skirt) could not just hang down; it had to "stick out." We wore these starched-stiff, ruffly slips in grade school (*before* uniforms). We had to be careful when we sat down, or people wouldn't be able to see our faces. Jean (who wore the most petticoats) remembers standing in the classroom aisle, putting her hands on the desk at each side—and swaying her skirt like a ringing bell, with her legs swinging back and forth like a clapper.

We had to be extra careful when we were playing that game where the rope gets higher and higher and you have to jump over it. A useful jump rope skill for petticoat wearers was the Judy J. Jump. This was named after a girl at our grade school who perfected a lightning-fast, sideways scissor kick to get over the highest ropes, wearing masses of petticoats, with minimal exposure. It should be noted that this is not a foolproof method. Once I noticed a small, bright yellow Band-Aid on her upper thigh. (It matched her scarf.)

Saddle shoes. These were clunky white lace-up shoes with a band of black or brown leather (that's the saddle part) wrapped around the middle of the shoe. (Diane's were brown with red rubber soles.) We wore these in grade school, but big girls wore them, too. There was a cartoon on TV with teenage chickens swooning and melting into their bobbie sox and saddle shoes when they heard their idol sing: "Ooooooh, Frankie!!!" (A very scrawny chicken with a large bobbing Adam's apple was supposed to look like Frank Sinatra. He was before our time, so this fad must have been pretty long-lived, too.)

Hula hoops. The hula hoop was a lot of fun (especially after we didn't have to share one hula hoop). Rumor had it you could "whittle your waist" so you would be all set to wear those shirtwaist dresses with big skirts and cinched-in-tight belts when you got older. (But when we got older the style changed to waistless dresses.)

Almost white lipstick. Did you just eat some ice cream or . . . are you okay? Do you have to *erpse*? Soon to be seen in our bathroom mirror!—*Susan*

Hula Hoop Economics

Hula hoops were a big fad when we were little. They cost $3.99 each when they came out, and Mom said we could only have one, because the price would go down for sure. So we got one red hula hoop and shared. *(It was really, really hard to share one hula hoop. There was "fighting."* —Susan) Darned if she wasn't right, because pretty soon hula hoops were $1.49, and we got a light blue one and a light green one. Eventually there were hula hoops everywhere, and they were even cheaper. Mom said this was "the law of supply and demand."

I still remember this lesson when the new flower varieties hit the market at ridiculous prices. I patiently wait, and what do you know . . . the price goes down.
—Jean

The Girls Dancing Club

When we were very little, we liked "How Much Is That Doggie in the Window?" (a grown-up song, with an "arf, arf" refrain), but as we got older, it sounded pretty silly. We sang along with Eddie Fisher's sentimental "Oh My Papa" and Doris Day's "My Secret Love." These were slow, slow songs, with lots of violins, and all the singers seemed to be our parents' age.

Then in 1955, when I was only seven, Bill Haley and the Comets sang "Rock Around the Clock" on the Ed Sullivan show (called *Toast of the Town* at the time), and music began changing a lot. Not long after this, our town's radio station, WOSH, became a Top 40 station (a new thing), and the songs we heard every day on the radio included more and more of the new rock and roll.

A TV show our family had been watching for years, *The Adventures of Ozzie and Harriet* (starring a real-life couple and their real-life kids, David and Ricky, who we saw grow up on the show), began to end each episode with a rock-and-roll song by Ricky and his band. Ricky Nelson's "Poor Little Fool" was the first rock-and-roll song I would admit to liking—because I knew Dad would tease me. (I heard it on *Ozzie and Harriet*!) I was in fourth grade and had just turned ten. My friend Maxine, in the same grade, was already an Elvis Presley fan.

Soon my sisters and I were turning on the TV every day after school to watch *American Bandstand*. This was music for *us*, and it made us feel like dancing! We stood on the living room carpet in front of the TV, trying to copy the dance steps done by all those cool Philadelphia teenagers. Often Patsy and Mary Lou came over and watched the show with us.

Patsy and I were the oldest, and we were *almost* teenagers. We couldn't just goof around—we really needed to learn these dance steps! That's how the Girls Dancing Club came about. Diane, Jean, and Mary Lou were recruited.

Our first official act as a club was to order special pencils, custom-printed with "Girls Dancing Club," from a cereal box. I have to take credit for being the genius who noticed that the initials of our club name were the same as the ones on the GDC (Guernsey Dairy Company) milk we were drinking. We cut out every GDC logo from the empty milk cartons—but never figured out how to use them (and they smelled a little sour). At our meetings we would practice the dances we had seen on *American Bandstand*. Did Patsy make a list of the dances using one of our official Girls Dancing Club pencils?

We watched *American Bandstand* for years. The cool Philadelphia teenagers' song rating, "It's got a great beat and you can dance to it," was how we felt about this show. We watched it so often that we could remember the names of those teenagers and kept track of when the couples broke up. Jean named one of the girls "Don't Know How She Does It," because she always had the cutest boyfriends and wasn't all that cute herself.

When Patsy, founding member of the Girls Dancing Club, finally became a teenager, we watched *her* on TV, dancing on *The Johnny Sax Show*, a local show that was just like *American Bandstand.*—Susan

Sister [Blank] the Nun (or Attila the Hun?)

I had a lot of really nice teachers in grade school: Mrs. Pfaffenroth, the perfect teacher in every way; jolly and fun-loving Sister Mary Albert; gentle Miss Kuble (our Aunt Dorie's sister); genial old Sister Gerard; and strict, but kindly, Sister Rachel. Of course, the exceptions make a much better story. (Certain names have been changed to protect . . . me.)

I entered St. Mary's School in first grade. Sister P—— was the first nun I ever saw up close, and it's pretty scary to see a lady with her head bandaged up tight, all covered with lots and lots of black material, when you're six. Even scarier than that, and this happened pretty often, she would turn sort of yellow and—thud!—she would pass out on the floor like she was dead, and one of the boys would run out and get a teacher. That kind of colored my experience of first grade, along with kids peeing in their seats (pee dripping off the seat and the mesmerizing little rivulet running down the aisle as you discreetly lifted your feet . . .), and being in the *second* reading group. We never found out what was wrong with gentle Sister P——, but she was healthy enough most days to be our teacher for the whole year. The charming (and healthy) Mrs. Pfaffenroth was such a delight for second grade that the girls wouldn't leave her side, even at recess.

The "star" of this story, Sister [Blank]—let's just call her Sister Attila—was my teacher in sixth grade. She was wiry and energetic with pointy black eyebrows, a sallow complexion, and a malicious toothy "smile." Whenever she was teaching us something, or telling us how horrible and how fat Sister Mary Albert was, we had to sit "Palms up. Feet flat." (Try this sometime, and please note that Sister Mary Albert was a big woman, but she was not fat, and we all liked her a lot.)

Sister Attila had a terrible temper and called us "fresh pieces of humanity" (the mild version) and "nasty pieces of humanity" (this was bad). To save time, sometimes we were merely "nasty pieces" or "fresh pieces." As the year progressed, almost all of the boys were hit or slapped on at least one occasion.

She chose me, unfortunately, to be her pet. She liked my handwriting and would hand me her class book so I could copy out things that I presume she was supposed to be doing. One of the things I had to copy was a list that I soon realized contained the IQ of everybody in the class, because the highest number was next to a boy she often told that with his IQ, he could do better.

Sister Attila also liked my artwork and had me do copies of details from famous paintings. (With crayons. Believe me, they weren't very good.) Art was her favorite subject. When it was time to hang up the class artwork, she had me

Mug shot of the former Teacher's Pet before she became a Fresh Piece of Humanity. Did this girl drop the pictures on purpose?

help her by holding up a drawing in each hand, so she could decide what looked good next to what. So there I am, standing in front of the class, and I accidentally drop one of the pictures. Sister Attila says, "You fresh piece of humanity. If you do that again, I'll hit you!" And guess what? I dropped it again. (Reflex action? I really didn't do it on purpose, unless subconsciously . . .) And she *hit* me. (Gasp from classmates.) Only one other girl had been hit by Sister Attila! And I was supposed to be her pet!

One day Sister Attila came in without the big toothy "smile" on her face. Later, when she accidentally opened her mouth too wide, we saw why. All her front teeth were gone! The class started giggling, and she spluttered out, "Haven't you ever broken a bridge?"—to sixth graders.

We were all happy to see the end of that year, and I hope by now Sister Attila has found the proper medication. There was a great esprit de corps among the members of that class, like buddies in a war zone. Whenever I run into anybody who was in that class, "Attila" inevitably comes up.—*Susan*

Goiter Pills, Anyone?

Friday was the designated day for passing out goiter pills at our grade school. Our teacher would haul out a huge dark brown glass jar of those chocolatey (chocolate flavoring was a sure bet to get most kids to actually look forward to this) confections—I mean, pills. A few kids (I won't name any names, but you know who you are) didn't like them and I bet wished they could offer them to those of us who did.

Back in the fifties, because of the rising occurrence of goiters (to those of you who aren't sure what a goiter is: as our Mother would say, "Look it up!"), health experts decided that the soil of the Midwest (referred to as the "Goiter Belt") didn't have enough iodine in it. The temporary solution for that problem was for schools to distribute iodine tablets, better known to many of us as "goiter pills."

Eventually iodine was added to table salt, which made goiters less common and goiter pills obsolete. Fridays just weren't the same anymore! If you were one of those goiter pill takers, you can probably still close your eyes, think real hard, and conjure up the scent and taste of those goiter-shrinking gems.—*Jean*

Ouch!

I don't know about you, but I remember tripping on the playground during recess and sprawling facedown, scraping my knees (with the skirt of my blue-plaid uniform jumper sailing up over my bottom side and covering my head, with my underpants in full view!) and wounding my pride. Nevertheless, I was led back into school by the supervising playground teacher, who I followed up the long narrow set of stairs over the entryway to the principal's office.

My wounds were cleaned up with soap and water, followed by a generous swabbing of Mercurochrome (I had to call my sister, Susan, the Spelling Champion, to find out how to spell that), which as I remember really stung! At any rate, with the covering of two Band-Aids, I was back out on the playground again to a chorus of "I saw London, I saw France. I saw Jeanie's underpants." Oh, shut up!—*Jean*

One day our friend Tommy ran up to us with a little white cardboard jewelry box—"Look what I found!" He opened the box with a flourish. We were horrified to see a severed finger resting on bloody cotton—until he couldn't resist wiggling it. He had cut a hole in the bottom of the box, dabbed the cotton with the rusty stain of Mercurochrome, put more on the base of his finger, and poked it through. Every scrape and cut was always painted with Mercurochrome.

The "mercuro" is for mercury—that's why you don't see little brown bottles of this stuff in the drugstore anymore. But I think Tommy's trick is still going around.—Susan

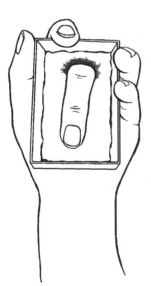

A nice, safe red marker can be used for dabbing "blood" on the cotton around the finger hole. (Be careful cutting the hole in the box or there'll be *real* blood on the cotton.)

The Carrot at the End of the "Stick"

For about eleven years I had to go to Dr.GuentherDr.Graber'sOffice (that's how they answered the phone) to get allergy shots. The waiting room smelled of medicine and rubbing alcohol. In the hallway was a drawer filled with those suckers with the soft loopy handles—Saf-T-Pops—to make little kids forget what had just happened.

After the shot, sometimes two, my arm(s) would get very hot and swell up where the needle had gone in. I had to sit in the waiting room for a while, until the nurse said it was okay to leave. When I was old enough to be there by myself, Mom would just drop me off. She never knew exactly what time to pick me up, so she had the excellent idea of having me wait for her in the Oshkosh Public Library, which was just around the corner from Dr.GuentherDr.Graber'sOffice.

Miss Malnar, the children's librarian, was there to guide me. (She read us a story about creamed angleworms on toast when she visited our grade school.

A postcard of the Oshkosh Public Library in 1935. It still looked much like this when I was getting my allergy shots nearby, but it was remodeled and expanded in 1967 (a few years after my shots ended).

I remember this every time I see soupy macaroni.) I checked out new books every week and read my way through the low shelves of the children's section (*Misty of Chincoteague, Little House on the Prairie* books, *Caddie Woodlawn* . . .). Several more years of shots went by, and I was over by the window exploring the juvenile section (Betsy/Tacy books, the Tippy Parrish series, *Seventeenth Summer* . . .).

When I was no longer given a Saf-T-Pop sucker after my shot(s), I moved on to the grown-up sections of the library, with its tall bookcases, reading rooms, and metal stairway to glass-block floors (craft books, magazines, all of Edna Ferber, Russian novels . . .).

Do I owe my love of books and libraries to allergy shots? Like Jimmy Hatlo said at the bottom of his "They'll Do It Every Time" cartoon in the newspaper: "Thanx and a tip of the (Hatlo) hat to . . ." Mom, for her *excellent* idea.—*Susan*

Thick and Thin: Our Grandpas

We had a fat grandpa and a thin grandpa. Grandpa Sanvidge (Victor Dewey Sanvidge, "Vic") was our thin grandpa. He was about five-foot-eight and 130 pounds (if that). Our fat grandpa was Grandpa Noffke (Henry August Albert Noffke, "H.A."). He was an inch shorter and more than double in weight: around 300 pounds at his biggest. Both grandpas had a sense of humor and their own businesses, and they both liked our Dad. Other than that, they didn't just look like opposites; they were opposites. (I'm going to start with Grandpa Sanvidge because he never would have put himself first.)

Both sets of grandparents usually came to our house for holidays. Grandpa Sanvidge has Jean and Diane on his lap, and Grandpa Noffke is on the couch.

Grandpa is sitting in his usual chair, wearing a tiny hat (a "gift certificate" for a new hat). He was also given an enormous cigar, which he pretended to smoke while still wearing the tiny hat, much to our delight, just after this picture was taken.

Grandpa Sanvidge

Grandpa Sanvidge was small-boned and olive-skinned with dark brown eyes that twinkled with amusement. His hair was always cropped short in a crew cut, and he wore a mechanic's uniform, gray, green, or brown, matching shirt and pants, most of the time. He was a meticulous, kind, and careful person who was good with his hands. Grandpa was a listener, a stamp collector, and a peaceful person to be with. Grandpa and Grandma Sanvidge married when he was eighteen and she was sixteen. Grandma could be a difficult person at times, but it was obvious to all of us that she always loved and respected Grandpa and that he felt the same way about her.

Grandpa Sanvidge worked as an engraver, developed machines to perform specific tasks, and then started his own business, Oshkosh Cutting Die. Making a cutting die involved inserting a sharp-edged blade from a continuous roll of blade-edged metal into precise grooves cut into a block of very hard plywood to provide a stamp for cutting out shapes, like unfolded boxes, odd-shaped greeting cards, or stick-on letters. Little square sponges were lined up right next to the cutting blade to pop the cut material off the die. You know those orange vinyl cones on roads to block traffic? When those were first invented, Grandpa was hired to cut out little cone silhouettes from the thick orange vinyl so his customer could mail out samples to cities. Grandpa gave us the scraps: circles with "spokes" made by the cut-out cones, and we used them like Frisbees. He always saved us scraps he thought we could use.

Oshkosh Cutting Die was in a building at the end of Grandma and Grandpa's driveway, next to an apple tree. We all remember the smell of well-oiled machines and fresh-sawn birch plywood in Grandpa's shop. Next to the door was an old Victorian engraving of a lady at a dressing table, and the picture looked like a skull from a distance. Beneath the engraving were the words "All is vanity." The shop was filled with jigsaws, presses, sanders, sheets of plywood, and shelves of rolled-up blades. Grandpa's office (where he also kept his stamp collection) was a few steps up, by a window.

Grandpa liked to go fishing and rarely caught a fish, but it didn't stop him from enjoying himself and didn't make him mad. He drove a bright turquoise Studebaker, a "modernistic" pointy car, which seemed unlikely for Grandpa (but not so unlikely for Grandma, who might very well have chosen it). Grandpa was a very good driver but had an amazing ability to get lost. Once I rode up to our cottage with Grandma and Grandpa, and somehow we ended up way east, in Mountain. Why didn't I say anything, when I had made that cottage trip hundreds of times? Because I thought we were going the right way. Grandpa passed his getting-lost trait on to me—along with his not-so-great-on-a-girl collarbones.

Grandpa Noffke

Grandpa Noffke was "a character." He was big-boned and bow-legged with an unusually large head, lots of wavy hair, blue eyes, and an ample curved nose. Grandpa spoke with a slight German accent, snorted, belched, smacked his lips, and really got into his food. He relished smelly food and enjoyed his schnapps. Grandpa wore lumberjack, woodsman, explorer clothes—thick wool and

An early photo of Grandpa Noffke (around the time he became a grandpa) in front of his coal yard, Noffke Fuel. The stone building at the left is the yard's office.

plaids—and was probably the only person in Oshkosh who wore a pith helmet while mowing his lawn (with a tractor and a farm implement).

He left home at age twelve (age seven in an alternate version of the story; Julie remembers hearing fourteen) and went to Chicago to be a hod carrier (carrying bricks and mortar to masons). He worked as a carpenter in northern Wisconsin, a building contractor in Appleton, and by the time Mom was ten, Grandpa had coal yards in three towns. He decided to keep the most profitable yard, the one in Oshkosh, and when he sold the other two, the family moved to Oshkosh. Noffke Fuel flourished, even during the Depression. As coal furnaces were starting to become scarce after the war, he changed his business to Noffke Lumber—just in time for the postwar building boom. Grandpa eventually owned a lot of land, a slew of rental houses, a cottage in Three Lakes, a house in Florida, and a farm "to putter around on." He had plans to build a shopping center (which he loved to talk about, *often*) on the big chunk of land he owned on Bowen Street up to Murdock, back as far as the train tracks. In the meantime, much to the dismay of the neighbors across the street, he bought a herd of cows and put the land to use. (Once we had to chase an escaped calf all over Oshkosh.)

For amusement, Grandpa played Skat, a very tricky old German card game for three people, with various cronies who smoked stinky cigars. I remember some of their names: Schuetzendorf and Bublitz, because they were so fun to say, and Harry Streich, because I threw up in his car (rainy day, closed windows, two cigars). Way back in the lumberyard Grandpa had a pen filled with howling hunting dogs (we could hear them from our house) that he would carry in the back of his none-too-clean, red-and-white International Scout. He liked to tease Grandma and Cile by drinking a big glass of cold coffee with ice, pretending it was whiskey. Grandpa Noffke's favorite chair in the living room was a sturdy, dark wood chair with lions' heads on the arms. It would not be difficult to picture Henry the Eighth in this chair.

Patience was not one of his virtues. Details were only a small part of the big picture for Grandpa Noffke (but he was very, very good at seeing the big picture). Once when Grandpa was tiling his bathroom, he called up our dad and asked him to come over right away. When Dad got there, Grandpa had bathroom tiles stuck all over his clothes, and the bathroom looked about the same as he did.

Grandpa Noffke did whatever he wanted, whenever he wanted—even when he was driving. When Grandpa wanted to look at something, even on Highway 41, he would slow to a crawl, paying absolutely no attention to the honking of all the other cars on the road. Once we were in the backseat (Never sit in the front!) of Grandpa's Cadillac as he drove down Murdock Avenue, with his head under the dashboard adjusting the radio, for at least two blocks. We ducked down behind the seats and prayed the Act of Contrition—just in case.

When we stayed at Grandma and Grandpa Noffke's house, Grandpa would drive us to church on Sunday. Most of the time he would stay in the car and read the Sunday paper. When he did come into the church, he would fall asleep immediately and snore really loud.—*Susan*

How to Make a Bottle Cap Fish Scraper

We grew up surrounded by rivers and lakes, and both our grandpas liked to fish. I remember seeing this homemade fish scraper when fish were being cleaned—on soggy newspapers piled with slimy innards, fish scales flying everywhere. (I can practically smell Grandpa Noffke's boat-house right now.) There were plenty of bottle caps around back then because beer and pop only came in bottles.—*Susan*

You will need:

- A piece of wood, about 1¼ to 1½ inches wide by ¾ inch deep and 10 inches long (it should feel comfortable to hold onto)
- Five metal, crinkled-edge bottle caps (the kind you need an opener to get off; if there's cork in them, pry it out)
- Flat-top upholstery or carpet tacks, or nails that are shorter than the thickness of the wood you're using
- A little upholstery or tack hammer

Nail down a single row of bottle caps—smooth side down, crinkled edge up—right next to each other, at one end of the stick. The other end will be the handle.

A note from the grandmas: Rinse well after using!

The Fourth of July

Uncle Cliff (our dad's brother) met our Aunt Millie in Georgia when he was there in the army, and that's where they raised our four cousins: Vic, Bert, Linda, and Ken. Every year around the Fourth of July, Uncle Cliff brought his family back to Wisconsin—a thousand-mile trip—all the way up without stopping to sleep at a motel.

"Are they there yet?" "Are they there yet?" As soon as Grandma's answer was yes, our whole family went right out to Grandma's to start one of our favorite parts of summer. Our aunt and uncle were as much fun to be with as their kids, and our parents always looked forward to their visit as much as we did. At first, the Wisconsin cousins and the Georgia cousins had trouble understanding each other's northern and southern accents. (Is it because of TV that it's not like this now?) We thought they talked funny; they thought we talked funny, and it always took a little time (and lots of mocking) to get used to this. Toward the end of the visit, we would find ourselves talking more like our Georgia cousins, but they would never admit to sounding more like us (Yankees).

Whenever the Sanvidge cousins got together (our Uncle Keith cousins, too), everything seemed to go outside of the rules. As the grown-ups sat around the

The cousins under Grandma and Grandpa Sanvidge's apple tree in 1958

picnic table talking, badminton birdies whizzed around them, nowhere near the net we had hammered into the ground. We would sit down at a card table to play poker, manage to play a few hands like normal people, and pretty soon, aces and kings were being stuffed in pockets, sleeves, and shoes, tucked under chairs, and sat on. "Y'all cheat!" (Laughter.) "Anybody need a 'tin' of hearts?" (Laughter.) We would start board games, and the hop-hop-hop from square to square would be enough to start us off laughing.

There was no barbecue grill at the many meals we ate together; most of the food was prepared ahead of time so there'd be more time to talk. Aunt Millie would fry up batches of her Southern Fried Chicken in Grandma's kitchen and bring out a big heap of chicken in a roaster pan. Reimer's hot dogs (made in Oshkosh; we all loved them) were the main course for multiple lunches and suppers, and potato chips were staples. Grandma made baked beans in her bean pot and an endless supply of her icebox cookies, and Mom would bring potato salad, homemade rolls or bread, and brownies or some kind of bars. We'd have a big bowl of cole slaw or pickles or cut-up carrots and celery, and there'd always be bottles of pop and beer in an ice chest. The main course for at least one of our meals was freshly caught fish. The Sanvidge men and boys all loved fishing, and they came back with perch, bass, and crappies from Lake Winnebago, Lake Butte des Morts, or Lake Winneconne near Uncle Keith's house (he had a boat), and Aunt Millie fried them up.

We usually managed to behave ourselves at the parade on Main Street in Oshkosh (always on July 4 no matter what day of the week it was), where we waved at Dad's friend and army buddy "Big Mike" marching down Main Street with the American Legion, and looked for people we knew. After yet another meal together, we would light a conservative collection of fireworks starting with those little tablets that erupt into twisting "snakes" of ashes. From that point on, soot smudges were part of our outfits. We tried to save our sparklers until dark.

Occasionally, as our boy cousins got older, a few contraband cherry bombs were exploded far enough away to diffuse the blame. (Celebrating the Fourth of July hasn't changed much, has it?)

When we were really little, going to the fireworks meant putting on our pajamas, crawling into the backseat of the car with blankets, and driving to Menominee Park (about six blocks away) to watch the fireworks over Lake Winnebago from the car. As all the cousins got older, we oohed and aahed over the fireworks from the roof of our garage. (This would never have happened if our cousins hadn't been there.) No matter what we did, we enjoyed being with each other.

All too soon came the day when our relatives climbed into their car to drive all the way back home, without stopping. In their trunk was the red ice chest that had chilled pop and beer for our picnics, now crammed with Reimer's hot dogs from Oshkosh to be eaten in Georgia.

Bert and I were very close and wrote to each other the rest of the year. As we all got older, Vic, our oldest cousin, stopped coming up, but Bert always came. He would stay at our house part of the time, and we'd all stay up really late. The summer before Bert went into the navy, he stayed at our house instead of Grandma's. We stayed up all that last night because we knew things wouldn't ever be the same.—*Susan*

Aunt Millie's Southern Fried Chicken

When I asked Aunt Millie for her Southern Fried Chicken recipe, she said, "You just *do* it." I did manage to pin down a *few* details.
—*Susan*

You will need:

A big deep frying pan
Fat or oil for frying: According to Aunt Millie, if you want this to be Southern, you should use lard, but Crisco or cooking oil is okay, too—for Northerners
Cut-up pieces of chicken
Salt
Self-rising flour in a shallow bowl for dipping (*Self-rising flour is a must.*)

Put the fat in the frying pan, turn burner to medium high, and keep an eye on the pan as it heats up while you lightly salt all the chicken pieces. There should be about a half-inch of fat or oil in the pan.

When the oil is hot, flop the first piece of chicken around in the self-rising flour to coat it, shake it off a little, and dip a little part of it into the oil. If a ring of bubbles forms around the edges or you hear a little sizzle, the oil is hot enough. (*Aunt Millie says "you just know" when it's hot enough.*)

Then "you just do it," dipping each piece in the flour just before frying it (on both sides), and as Aunt Millie says, "when it's done, take it out." (The rest of us will have to poke a fork into a thick part of the meat to see if the juices run clear—if pinkish, the chicken is not done.)

For "Southern Fried Fish"
Use cornmeal instead of flour, and salt after frying. The amount of fat in the pan will depend on the thickness of the fish you're frying. The rest of the process is the same as the fried chicken.

Aunt Millie says that lemons are served with fried fish in the South, but Uncle Clifford (a transplanted Northerner) used to make his own tartar sauce by adding diced pickles, dry mustard, and a little vinegar to mayonnaise.

Mom's Rye Bread

The week before our cousins came for their yearly visit, Mom did a lot of baking. There were tinfoil-covered 9-by-13-inch pans, tins of cookies, and rolls and bread stacked in the freezer. She remembers that Bert really liked this rye bread. Mom's Rye Bread is very good with Aunt Millie's Southern Fried Fish.

Makes two round loaves

You will need:

2 greased 8-inch pie plates or cake pans
2 cups warm water
2 tablespoons soft shortening (like Crisco)
2 tablespoons sugar
1 tablespoon caraway seeds
1 tablespoon salt
2 cups rye flour
1 (¼-ounce) package dry yeast
¼ cup warm water
4½ cups all-purpose white flour

Combine the 2 cups of warm water, shortening, sugar, caraway seeds, salt, and rye flour in a large bowl, and stir a little to submerge the ingredients. (Don't worry that the shortening has not melted.) Let stand five minutes.

Dissolve yeast in ¼ cup warm water, and stir into above mixture.

Work in white flour gradually, reserving ¼ cup to use later for kneading. Put dough on lightly floured board and shape into a ball. Cover with bowl and let rest for 10 minutes.

Knead for 10 minutes, put into greased bowl, cover, and let rise 1½ hours.

Punch down and divide dough in half. Cover, and let rest 10 minutes.

Shape each half into a round loaf and put in greased pans. Cover pans, and let rise 1 hour.

Preheat oven to 375° F. Bake for 40 to 45 minutes (until the top is nice and brown and snapping your finger on a loaf makes a hollow sound). Remove from pans to cool.

The Early Sixties

Susie got her first pair of "high" heels (if you can call 1 inch "high"), and Diane and I got Barbie dolls. Yikes! Our little baby sister Julie has learned to talk!—*Jean*

Dad's Desk

After Julie was born, our three-bedroom house was remodeled. A large room was added on the back, along with a much-needed "powder room," and Dad's old den became a bedroom for Diane and Julie. The new den was technically Dad's office, but it was also a guest room, dining room for parties, and a rec room—our blue-and-white hi-fi and sparse record collection (a "My Little Pony" cardboard record cut from a Wheaties box; a few red and yellow kiddie records; *Camelot* and *Sing Along with Mitch* albums; and two 45s, "Poetry in Motion" and "Red Rubber Ball") were tucked in a corner. In this room, Dad drew up plans for the houses he built and met with his customers in the evenings.

Dad's desk was a solid, practical piece of furniture that he built himself. His green desk chair was a standard office-type chair with entertainment value: it rolled, it spinned, and it rocked. A black Underwood typewriter and a check-protector stamping machine sat on a file cabinet near the window.

On the desk were a brown metal fluorescent desk lamp with intriguing on/off punch buttons; a pop-up address book with a little lever to choose the page you wanted (also intriguing); a totem pole pencil holder containing No. 3 yellow Ticonderoga lead pencils with green bands around the pink erasers and mechanical pencils with very thin lead you could shoot out by punching the end of the pen; a round ashtray that would spin the ashes around and dump them under a shield when you pushed the handle; a little brass stamp holder with a roll of stamps inside and one tempting stamp hanging out; and Dad's nemesis—the #!* telephone.

B-r-r-r-ing! B-r-r-r-ing!
"Dad, it's for you."
"[groan]"

A very good pencil sharpener, screwed to the corner of the desk, guaranteed we would be visiting Dad's desk very often.

Mom contributed a ceramic statue of Saint Joseph (the patron saint of carpenters) to Dad's desk. Saint Joseph's face had a suffering expression, as if he knew he was going to be meeting with customers when he was really, really hungry or when he would rather be watching *Gunsmoke*. Or maybe it was because he knew he was going to be glued back together many, many times. Or asked repeatedly—when Mom would make a novena (going to church nine days in a row)—to help sell the houses Dad did "on spec."

Dad's center desk drawer was a catchall. When Mom was neatening up the house, odd things, like my hairbrush, found their way into this drawer. When Jean was in her taking-apart-pens phase, Dad's desk drawer was filled with ballpoint pen pieces. If you couldn't find something in our house, it was always worth checking Dad's desk drawer.

One of the side drawers held *Neil V. Sanvidge, Builder* stationery and *Neil V. Sanvidge, Builder* pencils—white No. 3s with red printing on them.

Another drawer held stiff house plan books with plastic spiral bindings. Dad's customers would look at these, choose the house of their dreams, and ask him to change things a little—or a lot. He would pull out his drawing board with the sliding rule and his triangle, sharpen up a pencil, and draw up the plans. He had a transparent green template to trace in doors, sinks, toilets, and bathtubs.

I don't remember Dad yelling at us for scooting around the room and twirling and rocking in his green desk chair, pushing his lamp buttons on and off, popping his address book open and slamming it shut, taking his Ticonderoga pencils from the scary totem pole, shooting out the leads in his mechanical pencils, spinning his ashtray, unrolling his stamps, or dismembering his ballpoint pens.

I know he liked it when we were on the phone—he could watch *Gunsmoke* in peace.—*Susan*

"Dahling, I Need a Light"

Smokers were everywhere. Lucky Strike cigarettes sponsored a popular TV show called *Your Hit Parade*, a little bellhop yelled out "Call for Philip Mor-r-r-ris" on TV ads, and we were pretty sure our dad would walk a mile for a Camel. People smoked in restaurants, stores, and the hospital!

We copied movie stars, inhaling and exhaling with our candy cigarettes. "Dahling, I need a light." And we blew into the cardboard and foil play cigarettes to get a realistic puff of smoke to come out the end.

Ashtrays were part of our living room decor. There was a pair of tiny brass shoe ashtrays; little kids always tried to put them on, and nobody ever put ashes in them. We had a big glass and wood ashtray on the coffee table and a bigger one on a fancy stand with a handle so that it could easily be moved. Dad's office had a mechanical ashtray. We helped smokers by spinning their ashes away.

Dad smoked cigarettes for a while

"Dad, can I light it, please?"

and then switched to a pipe. He dipped tobacco right out of
the Prince Albert can (Yes, Prince Albert was in the can),
tamped it down with his pointer finger, and lit it with his
Zippo lighter. It smelled really good unless you were riding
in the car with the windows rolled up. We were always
"borrowing" his pipe cleaners for projects. . . . Be smart and
leave a few for Dad.—*Diane*

Dad and His Use of the English Language

I guess I've always paid close attention to what Dad had to say. When I was a
toddler, Mom walked into a room to find me playing "telephone" with the real
telephone and swearing a blue streak into it. I sure wouldn't have been imitating
Mom!

Dad had quite a few phrases that he'd use from time to time. When I find
myself using them now, people look at me like I'm from a different planet. I am.
I'm from Wisconsin! As you can imagine, coming from Wisconsin, Dad had
many phrases that had to do with cold weather. If someone left the door open
a little too long on a cold winter day, Dad might say, "Close that pneumonia
hole!" If he was the one coming in from the cold, he might say it was "colder than

Dad (at the right) with Edith and Roy Carpenter. What did Dad just say?

a well digger's ear" out there. A well-seasoned audience might hear that it's "colder than a witch's tit" or that "it's snowing like a bastard out there!"

Being a builder, Dad could appreciate a really fine or large home, saying, "That's quite a shanty!" Being a man, Dad could appreciate a really fine woman, saying, "She's built like a brick . . . ," well, you know the rest. He could also, even at his heaviest, notice a really large woman and comment, "Now there's a chunk of chocolate!" Our ever-kind Mom would then interject that the woman had a really pretty face.

Dad was a very patient father, but his patience did have its limits, and if we tested those limits, he might tell us that we "made his ass tired." I didn't know what that really meant when I was a kid, but I understand it completely as an adult. You do, too, and yes, you may use that phrase from now on.

Did Dad swear a lot? Only the generics passed his lips in front of us kids, but I'm sure things got more colorful around his friends. He once told a buddy that if he couldn't swear, he'd probably just explode. Jeez!

Dad liked to go out to dinner, and as we were leaving our car in the parking lot, he'd always admonish us to lock the doors because "there are a lot of white people here." He had heard a Menominee Indian say this in the parking lot when we went to a powwow on the reservation and he thought it was funny. If the meal was particularly sumptuous, Dad would comment, "I wonder what the poor people are doing tonight?" If you'd endeavor to pay and haul out your pitiful wad of one-dollar bills, he might ask you what you thought you were doing with that

"Michigan bankroll." (That's one of the phrases that make people look at me funny.)

He knew people since "Hector was a pup," thought people who lived together sans marriage were "shacking up," and called our car, any car, Nellie, and told it to "Whoa!" One of his first jobs was delivering ice with a horse and wagon, so I guess he came by that phrase honestly. If things were evenly divided, it was "a horse apiece."

> " . . . or I'll pound you in the ground."
> —Dad (to kids who were misbehaving)

Another time, I was telling Mom and Dad about a friend's financial follies, constantly teetering on the brink of bankruptcy, and that his mom bailed him out to the tune of several thousand dollars *again*. "She should have let him fry! He'll never learn anything if his mom keeps bailing him out!" I said, expecting that Dad would wholeheartedly agree.

He didn't.

He said, "Julie, no parent wants to see their child suffer."

Damn it, Pop—you're right.—*Julie*

Julie's Simple Pleasures

When we were kids, we made our own fun. Our dear parents were there to care for us, but they were *not* there to entertain us or be our playmates. We had hobbies and projects. We read books for fun. We played outside with neighbor kids. We spent time with our relatives and neighbors. We watched whatever was on our three measly TV channels, whether it was news, polka shows, old movies, or hunting shows. Going to the movies happened only a couple of times a year.

Were we deprived? Certainly not. We developed our imaginations, used

Julie playing dress-up with Mom's bridesmaid hat, just like her sisters did. There's an "autograph hound" on the top of the piano-that-Uncle-Keith-gave-us behind her.

our judgment, and enjoyed our creativity. As a result, we are resourceful, can-do girls, and I'm proud of that. So how did we while away the hours? Well, do you remember . . .

■ Pressing a pretty autumn leaf or spring flower in a heavy book, and the happy surprise of discovering it a few months later. Picking violets in the deep spring grass on the north side of the house. Rubbing dandelions on your cheeks to make them glow with yellow. Playing house in the woods, using a different rock for each room of your imaginary house.

■ Plucking peas in the pod from Dad's garden and eating them right there for a snack. Drinking water from Grandma and Grandpa's pump on a hot day. Playing in the sandy spot in the cottage driveway. Setting up a sand pie bakery amid the creeping phlox flowerbed behind the cottage.

■ Making Kool-Aid in the battered old aluminum pitcher. Freezing some in ice cube trays, using toothpicks for popsicle sticks. Chocolate pudding! Homemade ice cream. Tasting a buttercream rose from your birthday cake. Watching Mom make them. Dad's popcorn. Caramel corn. Thanksgiving stuffing. Campbell's tomato soup with a dab of melting butter on top and a grilled cheese sandwich on the side.

- Getting to sleep with Mom when Dad was out of town. Getting Mom to open her mouth so we could look at her teeth. Reading chapters of a good book with her at bedtime. "Now I lay me down to sleep . . ."

- Watching Mom get dolled up for a Saturday night date with Dad. Fashion shows with the Peters girls, using the cottage walkway as our runway.

- Shining Dad's shoes, and cleaning his pipes with pipe cleaners and putting in new filters. Making sculptures out of the pipe cleaners. Looking through the jewelry box that included his ribbons from World War II.

- "Helping" Dad at his work bench. Taking apart his ballpoint pens to see what was inside. (*And I always got blamed for that!—Jean*) Trying to fill his fountain pen with Shaeffer ink in the glass bottle with the little ledge inside. Tagging along with Dad to Grandpa's boathouse or squirrel hunting.

- Playing school with our authentic school desks (from Uncle Jim) and old readers (from Grandma Noffke). Rearranging our bedrooms to make them seem new again.

- Dressing our baby dolls with our own old baby clothes. Giving our dolls a bath in our play "bathinette." Washing our doll clothes.

- Paper dolls and coloring books. Collecting pretty rocks. Making potholders. Using pennies for tiddlywinks. Unwrapping crayons and using them to make a rubbing of something textured. Putting a blanket over a card table to make a hidey place.

- Wearing our spring clothes on the first nice day. (This was *way* after most of the other kids got to wear theirs!) Being fitted for a homemade dress, and the pins pricking us as we carefully removed it. Getting dolled up for Easter with a hat, gloves, and spring coat. A new holiday dress and tights for Christmas.

- Getting new shoes and school supplies every fall. Getting our favorite loafers resoled and putting shiny new pennies in them.

- Riding our bikes around and around the block. Using the oil can to keep them lubed up. Going to a firehouse in the springtime to get new bike license plates.

- Fizzies and sparklers after the Fourth of July fireworks. Raking the leaves in the yard into a kind of floor plan layout to play house. Marveling over the beautiful Jack Frost designs on the Bowen Street storm windows.

- Going to the fabric store to pick out new material for a wool quilt cover. Helping to put in the yarn ties, using a cardboard square to find the right spot.

- Grandma bringing over swatches of flannel so we could pick one out for our pajamas. Poring over Grandma's button box.

- Getting a crisp ten-dollar bill from Grandma and Grandpa Noffke every Christmas and birthday. Admiring the beautiful red roses Dad sent to Mom every year for their anniversary.

- Using our fingernails to scratch designs into the gummy varnish on the pews at St. Mary's. Taking Cheerios or Chex in our purses to church. Using the holy water fonts in our bedrooms. Wearing scapulars as a talisman against an early death! Pondering the *Lives of the Saints.*

- Reading Grandma Noffke's Time-Life books over and over—*Early Man, The Poles,* and *Five Days,* a book about the Kennedy assassination. Making a Christmas tree decoration out of an old *Reader's Digest.* Actually reading a *Reader's Digest* and *Life* and *Look* magazines.

- Practicing for our piano lesson with Miss Wille. (This is hard to remember, because we rarely did it.) Trying a new piano piece and always reverting to *Heart and Soul* and *Chopsticks.* Coaxing Dad to play his clarinet or harmonica.

- Going to nursing homes to carol at Christmastime. Taking tray favors and nut cups for other holidays.

- The fresh scent of our Scott Foresman textbooks. The smell of new crayons, Silly Putty, Play Doh, modeling clay.

This is a scapular. You put it over your head, like a necklace but under your clothes, with one holy card on your chest and one on your back. A bullet-proof vest for Catholics.

How to Make a "Decorative" Christmas Tree Out of a Reader's Digest Magazine

Grandma Noffke brought the *Reader's Digest* magazine to our house when she was done reading it. We turned it into high art for the holidays.

1. Carefully tear off the front and back covers.

2. Fold the first page forward so that the top edge is against the binding.

3. Fold the page again so that the fold you just made is against the binding.

4. Fold the triangle that hangs out the bottom up. That fold should be along the bottom edge of the book.

Repeat steps 2 to 4 until all the pages have been folded. Staple the first and last folded pages together to make the tree.

Spray paint your tree green or find some leftover flocking to decorate it. Grandma Sanvidge might have some from making her mirror look like it was in a snowstorm.—*Diane*

We weren't the only ones making these Christmas trees, and some people made Reader's Digest *angels.—Susan*

How to Make a Dandelion Chain

This is a fun thing I enjoyed doing on an early summer day when there were plenty of dandelions covering our yard and nobody was around to play with.

Find a basket, box, or container to put the dandelions in. Scout out all the dandelion flowers you can. Pick the dandelions, being sure to leave the stems attached. (Your parents will appreciate you for doing this, especially if you pick the flowers before they go to seed!) Pop off all the flower heads and get rid of them or give them to someone who likes to make Dandelion Wine like our Grandma did. (If they need a recipe, we have her recipe for it in our other book, *Apple Betty & Sloppy Joe.*)

Every dandelion stem has a wide opening and a narrow opening. Push the narrow end into the wide end to make a ring. Be sure to push it in there far enough so it stays together. Put the next stem through the first dandelion stem ring and form another ring the way you did the first one. Keep doing this until your chain is as long as you want it, then slip the last stem through the rings on both ends and connect it up.

Keep doing this until: it's time to eat; you've made a necklace, bracelets, and anklets for yourself and have run out of appendages to adorn (I'm sure your family would look lovely in them also); you've broken a record for the longest dandelion chain; or you run out of dandelions. (I'm sure your neighbors wouldn't mind it if you help yourself to theirs.)

—*Jean*

- Going for a Sunday drive. Stopping at a relative's to visit and listening to the grown-ups reminisce for hours at a time. Stopping at A&W on the way home from Grandma and Grandpa Sanvidge's for a "baby root beer."

- Getting on the bus all by ourselves and going to the library.

- Watching the apostles make their rounds on the Oshkosh Museum's clock.

- Getting ready for the fair and for 4-H food reviews.

- Knowing that I was really growing when I outgrew my blond "youth bed." I had to sleep on it diagonally for a few months until I could inherit a bigger bed from one of the big girls when they moved out.

I could go on and on, and I know you could, too.—*Julie*

Here I Am at Camp Hiwela

We joined the Camp Fire Girls at our grade school. (Jean was a year too young to be a Camp Fire Girl, so she had to be a Blue Bird.) There was a Camp Fire Girls camp, and one summer Mom and Dad signed up Diane, Jean, and me for Camp Hiwela, and Patsy and Mary Lou's parents signed them up, too.

You must bring everything on this list. And you must not forget your Camp Fire Girls kerchief or Blue Bird suspenders, a white blouse, and navy blue shorts.

Drive this way and that way through wooded and windy roads.

Walk through the hilly woods to your assigned cabin (and counselor). Your cabin is very primitive (but this *is* a camp), with twelve girls on six bunk beds.

Sign up for classes. (Wood-burning. Weaving plastic strips into bracelets. Making book covers from popsicle sticks. Beginners swimming.)

"You have to take a nap."

Dining Hall. Surprise! The food is really good. You can buy ice cream bars and Fudgsicles at the "canteen" with your own money. This might be fun ...

"You have to take a nap."

"You have to go to swimming class now, and you must wear this red cap so we know you can't swim." The campers in the blue caps are swimming and splashing, and the red caps (us) are standing in the lake, watching counselors show us how to swim. Our feet are sinking lower and lower into mucky sand. Fish are biting us! No, we are *not* imagining this! We

Here we are: Diane, Susie, and Jean, all packed up for Camp Hiwela. Julie will be able to play with anything she wants because we will be gone for a whole week.

are hopping up and down trying to keep the fish from nibbling our legs and toes. Nobody believes us. (Patsy got out of this. When she jumped in the water on the first day, she cut her foot. She *thought* it was a cut, but it was probably a *shark* bite. She is making lots of braided bracelets.)

"*You have to take a nap.*"

Diane's popsicle-stick book cover is finished. Her name is wood-burned on glued-together popsicle sticks. We all are wearing woven plastic bracelets. We still don't know how to swim. Mom sends us letters, but we can't read them. We walk all over camp trying to find someone who can read Mom's writing.

The cooks make homemade ice cream. It is excellent.

By now we know which counselors will let us read comic books while we're supposed to be taking a nap. We are really not tired at all. This place is run like a retirement home.

We prepare for the final event. (Patsy remembers weeding a field in the hot sun; I just remember being very hot in a big field.) After all the preparing, we have to put on our Camp Fire and Blue Bird outfits. There's a big campfire. We sing songs like "Wo-he-lo," "Michael Row the Boat Ashore," "Kumbaya," and our favorite, "Up in the Air, Junior Birdsmen." (Ask us to sing it. We still remember every word and gesture.) The next day we go home.

Mom and Dad probably got their money's worth in one way: being at the cottage looked pretty good to us for a while after this. We *never* had to take a nap there!—*Susan (with assistance from Patsy Lux and Jean)*

Angels on Horseback

"Oh, Wo-he-lo! Oh, Wo-he-lo!" Oh, what does that mean? WOrk-HEalth-LOve. This recipe is from the Campfire Girls handbook. We could earn a brown bead for camp craft, if Dad would let us use the grill.—*Diane*

1. Split a roll and insert a piece of cheese.

2. Wrap a piece of bacon around the roll.

3. Poke the end of a long sharpened stick or long-handled fork into the sandwich and toast it over a campfire until the bacon is done.

If your dad won't let you use the grill, you can make Angels on Horseback in the oven. Lay the sandwich on a cooling rack (so the bacon on the bottom will get crisp) and put that on a cookie sheet. Bake in a preheated 375° F oven until the bacon is done, 20 to 25 minutes.

Life before Panty Hose

Believe it or not, there was a time when panty hose did not exist.

Long ago, I made my First Communion. Mom made me a really pretty white dress, and we went to The Fatima Shop (a store with Catholic things like missals, rosaries, holy cards, and statues) to buy a communion veil. For the next part of the outfit, the nuns specified long white stockings, which were very difficult to find. (Not too many seven-year-old nurses around.) The last item was the most difficult to find: a tiny garter belt to hold up the white stockings. Mom finally found a pink garter belt, rippled with rows and rows of elastic, that was stretchy enough to fit a grown-up, but unstretched—it was small enough to hold those long white stockings up on a scrawny second-grader. After my First Communion, I was back in my Buster Brown ankle socks for five more years.

When I was twelve, it was time to join the big girls and wear nylons. Nylon stockings were sold folded and flat, in very shallow boxes. You had to buy the correct size because they barely stretched. When you held up a stocking you could see that your calf had better be in exactly the right place, too, because each stocking was shaped like a flat leg. Did I still have that stretchy pink garter belt somewhere? My first appearance in nylons, with blinding-white, bow-trimmed, very low "high heels," was greeted by this comment from my father:

"My girdle is killing me!"

> **"A woman has a right to a little belly."**
> —Aunt Millie

"Can you sing like a canary? You have legs like one!" I did.

Thinking about this now, I can't believe women put up with it for so long. What did ballet dancers wear? We never saw garters under their tutus. Why did it take so long for somebody to make the connection that whatever dancers were wearing just might work with nylons?

Fast forward to freshman year in college and the miniskirt. I'm sitting in a study carrel wearing a short dress—and a longish "panty girdle" just to hold up my nylon stockings—looking down in horror at the tops of my nylons showing and the ugly garters peeking out! This was 1967, and some entrepreneur's daughter must have had a similar experience, because soon after, panty hose came into being.—*Susan*

My sister Susan extolling the virtues of panty hose? Is this a fictional work?—Julie

Susan's Rebuttal: My little baby sister Julie loves to dress up. Like my father, I do not like to dress up, and I will wear nylons only when there is absolutely no alternative. Back then, it was pretty thrilling to feel like a "big girl," and now it's not.

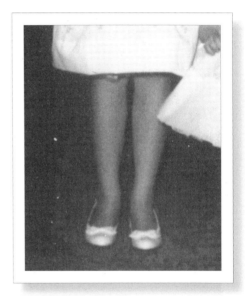

Well, I thought I had legs like a canary, until I found this picture of my actual sixth-grade legs in those terrible, blinding white shoes, proudly wearing my first pair of nylons (and probably that little pink garter belt). I had to restrain myself from doing a little retouching on this, because even though I weighed seventy pounds at the time, most of my weight seems to have pooled around my ankles.

The Opportunity

Along about the time I was in sixth grade (I think) and Diane was in seventh grade, Mom and Dad thought we should have our chance at music lessons. You see, Dad had a natural ability to play music "by ear," but when he was growing up, times were tough and his parents were more concerned with putting food on the table and a roof over their heads than providing music lessons. Not wanting to deny us the same opportunity, our parents signed me and Diane up to take piano lessons from Miss Wille.

Miss Wille lived on the south end of Bowen Street in Oshkosh, almost at the Fox River. After school, Diane and I would walk the seven or eight blocks from St. Mary's Grade School to her house. Miss Wille was a kindly, diminutive, gray-haired lady. Her house was small, with brown asphalt shingles. We would walk through the enclosed porch to the piano in her small living room.

Diane and I would take turns with our lessons and do our homework while we were waiting. Occasionally we would hear a male voice behind a curtained-off back room. The first time this happened, a cat walked out from behind the curtain and I thought Miss Wille had a talking cat! We found out later it was just Miss Wille's brother (probably talking to the cat).

As I remember, when it was my turn, I would flounder my way through "Betty and Bill" or some other selection I'd been assigned from Thompson's First Piano Book. I didn't particularly enjoy piano lessons and would usually only practice the night before our lessons. Miss Wille, probably sensing the futility of my musical future, would say, "Fine," stick on a gold star, and assign next week's song.

When are they going to stop that racket?

When Diane's turn came, she would play her piece through flawlessly, and Miss Wille would say, "I think you'd better do that one again for next week." Maybe Miss Wille knew there was more talent to challenge in Diane.

To this day, my only musical talents are in identifying tunes in a game that Dad liked to play with us (like the popular old show *Name That Tune*), naming songs on the car radio; and knowing a wrong note when somebody hits it. Unfortunately, I couldn't tell you the right one.

Despite *my* lack of musical talent, I sure did enjoy listening to Dad play his harmonica and clarinet, which sounded great—and *he* didn't even have lessons!—*Jean*

By the time Julie was taking piano lessons from Miss Wille, the B-flat key on the old piano from Uncle Keith had broken, and she had to hum it.—Susan

Duck-Duck

To show us the Miracle of Birth (the more interesting parts of that story we "learned" via a marginally informative book for teenagers written by a reverend/ minister who was on TV—tossed into our room by our mother, who then fled), Mom bought a quail egg incubator and quail eggs. She put it on the yellow linoleum kitchen counter (right under the cereal cupboard!) and plugged it in. The eggs were on their way to becoming baby quails when I accidentally knocked it over and the eggs broke. Apologies to Mom (and the future quails)! That's how we happened to have an egg incubator at our house.

One spring Dad brought a mallard duck egg home and put it in Mom's incubator. This time the incubator (lightweight plastic) was put in a safe place where it wouldn't get bumped: the fireplace, of course.

We checked the incubator often, and one day we saw a crack in the egg. Jean and I watched as the crack widened. A dark and soggy head popped out, then a skinny neck stretched wa-a-a-ay out, and Duck-Duck looked right at us, sideways, with just one of his bright little eyes.

Duck-Duck (never officially named) would not let us out of his sight. His home was a cardboard box in the kitchen, furnished with a pink plastic hand mirror in a futile attempt to convince him that he was a duck. He was fine with being in the box as long as he could hear us talking. As soon as we started leaving the kitchen, he would back up as far as he could in the box, start running, jump onto the flap of the box, slide down on his little behind, and follow us out of the room.

His eyes were a little like Grandpa Sanvidge's—very dark brown with a look of intelligence and amusement. Duck-Duck would tilt his head to listen to us, and he had a muted little quack.

We filled the bathtub with water so Duck-Duck could swim, and he dove for the food pellets we threw in, his stumpy tail wiggling. Julie remembers him "diving for frozen peas and sometimes his own poo." (He left little poops in the bathtub. I can't believe Mom let us do this.) Once he ate a cigarette butt and walked around like a little drunk until he pooped it out. When we took him outside, he was determined to follow us everywhere, even if we ran.

All good things must end, and Duck-Duck, the much-loved house duckling, started sprouting his flying feathers. (We always thought of Duck-Duck as a male, so when "his" feathers came in as *female* mallard brown, it was too late to think of him as a "her." We should have known—we only have girls in our family.)

As Duck-Duck sprouted more and more feathers, it was time to look at him (her) through Mom's eyes: a soon-to-be adult duck who could fly anywhere in the house—leaving a trail of . . . (Mom: *six* quails?)

Dad talked to a friend who said he'd take Duck-Duck to his farm. Dad's friend put Duck-Duck in with geese, which are known for being aggressive, but we heard that Duck-Duck held his own. He thought he was a human. We all loved that little duck.

We were always afraid to ask what happened after that, and I can tell you that it would be a long, long time before Susie the Picky Eater would eat roast duck again.—*Susan*

Do You Want to Go to Heaven?

Religion was an important part of our growing-up experience. Dad wasn't raised Catholic, but when he and Mom decided to get married, Dad agreed to convert. (In those days it was an important issue for the Church that both spouses be Catholic.)

We went to Mass as a family every Sunday at St. Mary's Catholic Church on Merritt Avenue and were all sent to St. Mary's Grade School. Every weekday before school started, we went to Mass, and the Sisters of St. Agnes taught us how to be good Catholics. We learned a few other things, too . . .

Childhood Memories of Being Catholic and Going to Church

- *Mandatory Hats*: If you forgot your hat or mantilla, you had to wear a hankie on your head. (*Or a washcloth: Grandma Sanvidge once fashioned hats for us from threadbare washcloths when Mom had forgotten to bring our hats up to the cottage. I remember thinking they were really nice. They couldn't have been.—Susan. Or a "chapel cap!" This was a round, lace "doily" in a portable plastic packet.—Julie*)

Oshkosh Northwestern

"Seen at Early Easter Service—Mrs. Neil Sanvidge, 944 Bowen St., brought her three daughters, from left, Susan, Diane and Jean, to the early-service at St. Mary's Catholic Church Sunday morning." From the *Oshkosh Daily Northwestern*, April 11, 1955.

- *Act of Contrition*: I remember saying the Act of Contrition in the backseat of Grandpa Noffke's Cadillac because I wasn't sure I'd make it home alive.

- *St. Anthony*: If you pray to St. Anthony when you lose something, you'll find it. I've taken advantage of this so often, I'm sure St. Anthony will be expecting me to help him out when I get to heaven.

- *Confession*: Sure hope those people in line can't hear me!

- *First Communion*: You're supposed to stick out your tongue. ("Mom, I thought we're not supposed to do that!") The host sticks to the roof of your mouth!

- *Going to Church Alone*: Put a Kleenex in your pocket! I remember having to blow my nose so bad that I contemplated ripping a page out of my Daily Missal to take care of it.

- *Lent*: This is always Dad's time to diet, and our time to give up candy.

- *"Offer It Up!" (for the Poor Souls in Purgatory)*: What Mom always says when things are not going your way.

- *Sister Rachel, Sister Gerard, Sister Mary Bernard*: A great principal, and two of my favorite teachers

- *Bishop Grellinger*: A very holy man

- *Father DuCharme*: A very good-looking priest

- *Sister DeChantal*: We thought she should marry Father DuCharme. (*My fourth-grade class thought he should marry* our *teacher, Miss Kuble.—Susan*)

- *Girls Sodality Group*: There were trips with the nuns. "Mom, are you sure you want to drive? You got lost last time."

- *Bats flying down the aisle during the sermon*: "Mom: Grab your hat, and duck!"—*Jean*

A Few Irreverent Comments about Church

Warning: The following may not be appropriate for seriously religious readers.

- *Knee Bump Syndrome*: After years of Catholic school and going to Mass every single morning before school, my sisters and I all had little bumps on our knees. We discovered that inside each bump was a very fine, coiled hair. This condition, which I am convinced was from kneeling six days a week (counting Sunday Mass), for at least forty-five minutes, miraculously cured itself when we went to high school, where daily Mass was not required.

- *Pagan Babies*: Grade school kids would scrape together pennies and nickels until they had five whole dollars, which bought the right to baptize, and name, a child somewhere in the world. Julie saved up five dollars all by herself, and somewhere in the "Far East," there is a forty-year-old man named Avery Olan—a combination of Julie's favorite name at the time and the main (female) character in *The Good Earth*. He may not like his name much, but Julie did save him from an eternity in Purgatory.

- *Sucking Cough Drops in Church*: You have to be a very old nun, with a very bad cough, to get away with this.

Tips for Surviving Long Sermons and High Mass

1. If you aren't fasting to go to communion, make sure not to chew your breakfast too thoroughly. And don't brush your teeth either. There is a lot of entertainment value in finding those little pieces of eggs and toast.

2. Take one of those fat missals with you. There are stories about the saints for every day of the year in the back. (Check out July 17: St. Alexius. What a story! While you're paging through the stories, see if you can find one married woman saint who isn't a widow.)

3. Put interesting things to look at in your purse. Almost anything will be interesting enough.

4. Look at every single detail on your church envelope, your fingers, your coat, and the neck of the person in front of you.

5. Think about Sister Elvis (or was it Alvis, maybe?), our grade school principal for a very short time in the late 1950s, and how she feels about her unfortunate name choice.—*Susan*

"I *am* nothing but a hound dog!"

I Was Mary in the Christmas Play

In eighth grade, the nuns chose me to play Mary in the annual Christmas play at St. Mary's School. They must have chosen me because I had longish hair and didn't wear glasses (at the time). For Joseph, the nuns chose a boy in my class who was not exactly the obedient, religious type, so I know holiness had nothing to do with it.

We were supposed to look like this holy card from my First Communion prayer book.

I was on the stage for the entire play but fortunately had only three lines to memorize. ("Joseph, there is no room," was one of them.) Baby Jesus was mysteriously and painlessly born at some point behind those dusty velvet curtains, in the form of the smallest third-grade boy the nuns could come up with. They must have thought second-graders were too unpredictable.

The curtain opened. Joseph and I were kneeling piously with our hands folded, gazing down at a rickety, oversized manger made of two-by-fours, holding an eight-year-old named Charlie. His wiry little form was swaddled precariously in a white sheet, and he was flailing his arms and legs around in a hyperactive third-grader's imitation of a newborn—while blinking his eyes at lightning speed and darting his tongue in and out like a lizard.

It was very hard to look holy.—*Susan*

We Saw It on TV

I don't remember watching the news much. I know Mom was a big fan of the *Today Show* and Hugh Downs, but we were always at school or playing when that show was on. We heard about the nasty Nikita Khrushchev and knew Eisenhower was the president. We heard about the beginning of the space race—Russia beat us to the punch by launching Sputnik II before we launched Explorer I. Elvis got drafted. Alaska and Hawaii became states.

Then came 1960. The handsome John Kennedy was running for president. Kennedy was Catholic, young, and very popular with the nuns at St. Mary's. They held pre-election voting for the students. ("Vote like your parents.") Kennedy won by a landslide at our school.

Ask anybody who lived through it what they were doing November 22, 1963, and they can tell you immediately. I was in the basement of St. Mary's Church, helping Sister DeChantal clean the altar. A student came in and said that President Kennedy had been shot. Everyone went back to their classrooms and waited for more news. Later it was announced that he had died.

We watched TV that weekend nonstop. They played the motorcade scene over and over: Jackie's pink suit with the blood on it. Lee Harvey Oswald arrested. Lyndon B. Johnson taking the Oath of Office.

On Sunday morning we all got ready to go out to eat with Grandma Noffke. The TV was still on. As we were putting our coats on and standing there gazing at the TV, we saw Jack Ruby shoot Lee Harvey Oswald right there on the TV. *Live*, as it was happening.

We watched President Kennedy's funeral, broadcast live, too, and saw little John John salute his father's casket.

We all grew up that weekend, and things would never feel the same again.
—*Diane*

Skaters Waltz and Crack the Whip

Every winter, the playgrounds of all the public schools in Oshkosh were flooded to make ice rinks, and each one had a "warming house" inside the school, with pieces of plywood on the floor so our skates wouldn't damage it. There was always an adult there, and at closing time, when we went in to take off our skates, he would spray the ice with a big hose to make it smooth again for the next night. We were dropped off and picked up at the Dale School rink until Emmeline Cook School near our house had a rink, too. It was close enough (and we were old enough) to walk there all by ourselves.

Jean and I loved to skate, and we walked to Emmeline Cook many winter nights. (Our record was nine nights in a row.) Music was piped over loudspeakers, and the rink was softly lit, surrounded by banks of snow. In the early part of the evening we would see accomplished skaters doing figure-eights and twirls, couples with arms entwined skating serenely to the music, and little kids on double-runner skates slipping and skidding and trying not to fall.

This group left early, and the remaining crowd (including us) was more into skating really fast, jumping into snow banks, and getting kids together for playground games that were supposed to be played in shoes. We couldn't have played Crack the Whip very often because we don't remember injuries (a faint memory of someone's blood-rimmed tooth?). Coyote was the game we played the most. I only remember that it was kind of like football, without the ball, on ice, wearing skates—but Jean remembers how to play Coyote and she will give you the details after her story. —*Susan*

■ ■ ■

I remember one particular beautiful winter night of skating at Emmeline Cook when the conditions were just perfect. They were so perfect, in fact, that unbeknownst to us, Mr. Behlman, the rink custodian, decided to keep the rink open a half hour longer than usual. I don't remember if Susie or I had a watch on—even if we did, it was too dark out there at night to see it anyway.

When the lights on the rink went out (the signal for closing time), Susie and I headed into the warming house, our skates cutting into the plywood boards used to protect the floors, and plopped down on the benches to take off our skates. Susie and I said our good-byes to our friends and walked the four and a half blocks home.

Mom's frantic worry ("Where could they be? The rink closed over a half hour ago!") turned to relief at the sight of us ("There you two are!") to fury ("Where have you been and why are you so late?"). Since we were totally oblivious to the fact that we were even late, Susie and I were dumbfounded! You know how ignorance is no excuse when it comes to breaking civil laws? Well, it didn't work with Mother's Laws either. We were grounded, but good—no skating at Emmeline Cook for *two weeks*! But, Mom . . .

I loved ice skating so much that I had brief delusional ambitions of being a professional skater. I entered a speed skating race one winter that was held at Menominee Park in Oshkosh and even got to meet Maddy Horn, who was a 1938 Olympic silver medalist in the Women's 500- and 1,000-meter speed skating. I got a disappointing third place (I still have the ribbon) in my age division and figured out that speed skating wouldn't be my claim to skating fame.

One winter, when I was in about seventh grade, Mom and Dad took our family for a special outing up to the Green Bay Arena for a "Holiday on Ice" performance. I was mesmerized and enthralled at the skill, grace, and ability of those wonderful skaters and thought surely I could do that, with enough practice, of course. It didn't take long for my confidence to be totally dashed when out skated a young boy and girl who were about half my age and who could perform feats on their skates I couldn't begin to do. I realized then and there that it was too late for me to even *think* of becoming a professional figure skater.—*Jean*

How to Play Coyote (on Skates)

To play Coyote you need to be a good ice skater. The game can get rough at times. It was usually played after most of the other younger skaters had left the rink.

A person stands in the middle of the ice rink (usually one of the bigger kids, probably the one who came up with the idea of playing the game). That person is the Coyote. The rest of the players stand in a line facing the Coyote along one edge of the rink.

At the Coyote's command the line of skaters tries to race past the Coyote, while he or she tries to tag as many kids as possible. The kids who are tagged have to join the Coyote in the middle, in a line. The kids who didn't get tagged skate at them from the opposite edge of the rink this time.

The game continues until there is only one person left. That person is the winner and will be the Coyote in the next round.—*Jean*

I Learned to Dance at Catholic School

Rock and roll was such a big deal that it even infiltrated *Catholic* schools. From grade school through high school, between fractions and prepositions, religious instruction and frog dissection, we were given a daily dose of rock and roll—and an opportunity to dance. Apparently the nuns thought we should be learning about "temporal life," too.

Dancing at St. Mary's (Catholic) Grade School

After eating Mrs. Boehm's memorably soupy macaroni and cheese, chewing bright squares of sturdy Jell-O, and draining our little glass bottles of GDC milk in the school cafeteria (with very thin straws), we would go into a big, low-ceilinged activity room next to the cafeteria. The big girls, seventh and eighth graders, would bring their favorite records to school, and the Sisters of St. Agnes—*nuns*—supplied a record player! Yes, they did—and I remind you that this was St. Mary's Catholic Grade School. Believe it or not, almost all the girls (never the boys) danced to rock and roll every lunch hour. In fourth grade, I had "rock-and-roll saddle shoes." They were white with a black saddle-shoe band that came to a point on either side of the laces, and the soles were soft and smooth—perfect for dancing.

As our eighth-grade graduation approached, the nuns felt that we were about to be launched into high school—and we really should know ballroom dancing (a bit of a generation gap here). A note went home about a class offered at Richard's School of the Dance, and nearly the entire class signed up. We learned how to dance the waltz, the fox trot, the lindy, and the cha cha. I won the first prize for the girls and got a little plastic trophy that I still have somewhere. Tommy Wrchota won the prize for the boys. Every class reunion, we can't help bringing this up. I bet he still has his trophy, too.

Dancing at Lourdes (Catholic) High School

Lourdes was a completely different school on the other side of town, and the School Sisters of Notre Dame were our teachers, but guess what we did after lunch? We (girls only, again) danced to rock-and-roll records—as the boys watched—every day after lunch. Oddly, the nuns seemed to think this was perfectly okay. Our principal *(whose name is not mentioned here "to protect the 'Innocence'"—Jean)*, a strict and serious nun whose pronunciation of the letter *P* over the school intercom was notably explosive, was all for it, too. Once, when she was primly announcing the details of an upcoming dance over the intercom, she added that a local disk jockey would be there (pause as she looks down to read—here come those *Ps*) . . . "to spin the platters."

Yes, it's true that I learned the shuffle-ball-change and the shuffle-hop from my friend Patsy, was one of the founding members of the Girls Dancing Club, and watched hours of *American Bandstand*. I guess what I really learned at Catholic school was how to dance and not feel the least bit self-conscious about it, because the *nuns* were behind it 100 percent.—*Susan*

How to Dance the Mashed Potato

"It's the latest; it's the greatest . . . Mashed Potato, yeah, yeah, yeah . . ."
When Dee Dee Sharp's "Mashed Potato Time" starts playing, I will be dancing no matter where I am.

Remember seeing people do the Charleston and how their feet take turns doing half-swivels with heels a little off the ground, while moving back and forth?

Doing the Mashed Potato is very much like that, but as your feet take turns swiveling (or "mashing") you shift from foot to foot *in the same place.* Your body will be swaying from side to side a little (to help you keep your balance), and a little leading-with-the-shoulder move is going to come along with that sway when you really get into the music.

Instead of the stiff arms and splayed fingers of the Charleston, your arms should be relaxed and bent slightly at the elbows, moving in and out in time to the music—like chicken wings, trying to get the chicken off the ground.

Once you get the movement down, you may find yourself moving around a little, in circles, or mashed-potato-ing your way across the gym floor to where that cute guy with the blue eyes is standing . . . —*Susan*

"(Oh Baby) Meet Me on South Street . . ."

"Oh yeah, hurry on down . . . the hippest street in town."

The other dancing fiend in the house was Diane. We had to do dishes every night, and tuning the radio to the Top 40 hits on WOSH made everything go faster. We *did* have a dishwasher (but you might as well wash them by hand after you're done with all that scraping and rinsing), and it was so dreary doing those pots and pans that, dishtowels in hand, we danced while we did the dishes.

The song "South Street" always sent us flying down our long hallway, dishtowels flopping to the beat.

"*West Street, East Street, North Avenue . . . South Street's the best street . . .*" to do dishes with you!—*Susan*

How to Make a Gum Wrapper Chain

We didn't dance *all* of the time—we had other obsessions to attend to. This one is a masterpiece of time wasting. (Is your homework done?) We chewed a lot of Juicy Fruit, but it was "really neat" if you had a variety of wrappers. Beeman's and Clove gum were big favorites of ours, but we had to ask Dad to save his Black Jack gum wrappers—it was licorice flavored, and we didn't like it at all.

We have it from a reliable source (my little pink diary from freshman year in high school) that Diane's gum wrapper chain was 64½ inches long on March 12, 1963, when mine was only 13 inches. After only two more months of diligent chewing, my gum wrapper chain was 69½ inches long.

Diane's going to tell you how to make one.—*Susan*

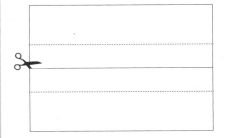

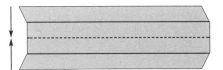

1. Fold the gum wrappers you've collected (the paper wrappers, not the foil) in half lengthwise, and tear or cut along the fold to make each one into two pieces. If you're not a gum chewer, you could cut 1-inch by 3-inch strips of origami paper or not-too-flimsy printed wrapping papers (and go to step 2).

2. For each piece: With the printed part on the outside, fold in half lengthwise and then open again to lay flat.

Continued on next page

3. Fold in each long side so the edges meet at the center fold.

4. Fold in half lengthwise at the center fold. (You should have a 1/4-inch strip, no raw edges showing, four layers thick.)

5. Fold the strip in half widthwise into a "V" shape. through the loops of the other.

6. Open the "V." Fold each end of the strip in to meet at the inside fold, and fold again at the center. (You should now have a smaller "V" shape, eight layers thick.)

7. Do the same thing with the other wrappers. To connect the pieces, push the ends of one "V" through the loops of the other.

8. Repeat. Repeat. Repeat. Until your chain is really long.

Veni, Vidi, Edi (I Came, I Saw, I Ate): Our High School Cafeteria

Our high school cafeteria was a sunny, low-ceilinged room with the usual lunchtime scraping of chairs and chatter, but to graduates of a certain era, it was unforgettable.

The Lourdes High School cafeteria was the setting for a "Roman Banquet" conjured up by our vivacious Latin teacher, Sister Margaret Ann. (All girls— the boys had separate classes.) Latin II, III, and IV students, draped in bed-sheet togas, presided over long Formica tables, eating food with their hands and calling out orders to barefoot Latin I student "slaves" sprawled on the floor in frumpy gym suits (with snaps and *bloomers*). After the feasting came the fun: Sister Margaret Ann had translated popular song lyrics into Latin, and she handed out purple mimeographed sheets for a lively dead-language singalong. One of the songs was Buddy Holly's "Peggy Sue": *Pegia Suna, Pegia Suna, pulchra, pulchra, pulchra, pulchra* . . . Who could forget that?

Besides the annual Art Fair and an occasional dance when the gym floor was being refinished, our cafeteria was also the scene of a festive lunchtime birthday party my friend Nooker (a.k.a. Kathleen Mary Laverne Baier) put together for me—an event that involved a big green glass bottle of 7UP, laced with her dad's Cherry Kijafa (16 percent alcohol), in the midst of pastel cafeteria trays. And cake, too, of course. (We were not caught, and my mother is hearing about it for the first time here.)

But what *everybody* remembers, and brings

The Cherry Kijafa Incident as commemorated in a multipage birthday card I made for Nooker twenty-six years later.

up the moment you mention the cafeteria, is the food. The kitchen was at the east end of the room—all chilly-looking tiles and stainless steel equipment, like cafeterias everywhere—but that's where ordinary stopped. Behind the stainless steel tray slide stood our cafeteria's special ingredients: three calm, smiling, motherly ladies in print grandma-aprons, Mrs. Schertz, the head cook, and her assistants, Mrs. Radley and Mrs. Heil. These cheerful ladies cooked for eight hundred teenagers as if they were feeding their own grandchildren: no amount of effort was too much.

Just-like-home main courses included scalloped potatoes and ham *(Don't forget the meatloaf! I always asked for two helpings.—Jean)*, hamburger and rice casserole (my favorite), and pigs in a blanket (everybody's favorite): pork sausages, individually wrapped in fragrant, freshly baked bread, with the juice from the sausages oozing into it. Oh my, I could go for some of those right now.

Mrs. Schertz and her cohorts did all their baking *from scratch*. Still-warm delicate cinnamon rolls with melting dribbles of frosting; crumbly, tart cherry cobbler; lavishly frosted "Chicagos" (a.k.a. long johns), and grophens—raisin-studded, sugar-encrusted, raised doughnuts with a chewy dent in the middle—were among the treats that graced our melamine trays. Nooker remembers sweet rolls: "Huge sheets of them. Not too much cinnamon, light sweet icing, and *toasted* coconut on top." I remember that even the buns on the sloppy joes were especially good, and the ladies must have made those, too. Very few kids brought bag lunches to our high school cafeteria, and when certain familiar aromas wafted down the halls, they chucked their bag lunches in the trash and got in line.

Not too long ago, Diane was rhapsodizing about Mrs. Schertz's grophens to one of our Lourdes' classmates, the former Judy Ostertag, who happens to be married to Mrs. Schertz's grandson, and Judy said, "I have that recipe and I can show you how to make them."

Let's raise a grophen (or a couple dozen) to Mrs. Schertz!—*Susan*

Mrs. Schertz's Grophens

Mrs. Schertz's original recipe uses 10 cups of flour and makes about 24 hefty grophens (multiply that for 800 kids!), and her instructions are aimed at experienced doughnut makers. We halved Mrs. Schertz's recipe and added details in brackets for inexperienced doughnut makers—which included us. The grophens turned out great the first time we made them, and yes, we still like them as much as we did in high school!—*Susan, Diane, and Jean*

Makes 12 to 14 grophens

You will need: a heavy-duty pot or kettle for deep frying and metal tongs. A deep fry thermometer is very helpful.

1 ounce yeast cake [which comes in 2-ounce packages; or 1½ packages dry yeast—half-package is 1⅛ teaspoons]

½ teaspoon sugar

¼ cup warm water

½ stick oleo [margarine; that's ¼ cup, or 4 tablespoons]

1 cup scalded milk (2% or whole milk, not skim)

1½ teaspoons vegetable oil

5 cups flour

¼ cup sugar

½ teaspoon salt

½ cup dark raisins

3 eggs, beaten

Vegetable oil for frying [1½ inches deep in pot]

[Granulated sugar for coating]

Continued on next page

From the Kitchen

Dissolve yeast with ½ teaspoon sugar in ¼ cup warm water. Soften oleo in scalded milk. [Let cool to lukewarm.]

Mix well all ingredients in container with [1½ teaspoons] vegetable oil in bottom [first the flour, sugar, salt, and raisins, then stir in milk/oleo combined with beaten eggs and yeast]. Mix to a stiff dough but still sticky and smooth. Let rise until double in bulk [covered, 2 to 2½ hours].

Form into balls about the size of a doughnut cutter [2 to 2½ inches across; grease hands with vegetable oil to handle the sticky dough]. Let rise about ½ hour.

[Heat the vegetable oil, 1½ inches deep in the pot, to 350° F—a 1-inch cube of bread will brown in 1 minute.]

Shape by thinning the center with fingers [poking and stretching a deep well in the dough ball as it sits on a cookie sheet: it should look like a wide doughnut with about ⅛-inch-thick dough across the "hole"] and fry in deep hot shortening until golden brown—turn and fry the other side—drain on paper toweling. Can be sugared. [Mrs. Schertz always sugared the doughnuts she made for us at school. Since you're not making 800 grophens you could put sugar in a paper bag and as the grophens are fried, put each one in the bag and shake to coat it.]

Nooker's Aunt Helen also made grophens. She fried them in her basement (it can be messy) and always wore a shower cap to keep her hair clean. You might want to try that.

Mom: The Exposé

The inside scoop by her oldest daughter, Susan

More than anybody else, our mom runs like a thread (good, strong buttonhole twist) through our stories. You probably have a pretty good picture of her by now—as she would describe it, "warts and all." Which reminds me, we didn't tell you about the huge wart she had on the side of her thumb. Uncle Jimmy suggested burying a potato under a full moon, and I'm really not sure how she got rid of it, but she did.

A word Mom uses a lot is *gumption*, and the various meanings of this word—good common sense, willingness to take the initiative, and a fighting spirit in the face of difficulty—are a description of her character.

Mom's strongest expletive is "I could just spit!" (and a little of that spit on the corner of a handkerchief cleaned our smudged faces away from home). When anything fun is going on, Mom is in for the duration—she doesn't want to miss anything. When something strikes her as funny, she will be *consumed* by laughter to the point of gasping for air.

Our mother has always been interested in politics and loves talking about it. (Our dad did not love talking politics, and because of this, Dad never, ever, not even one time, would tell us who he was voting for.) When we brought boyfriends home to meet our parents, the ones who liked to discuss politics always chalked up points with Mom. I once

Our mother, Helen Noffke Sanvidge, in the mid-1960s

(*only* once) went out with a guy who got into such a lively political discussion with Mom that I had to drag him out the door.

Mom doesn't just talk about things, she stands up for what she believes in, and she's been an organizer, organization starter, activist, petition-circulating conservationist, and recipient of many awards. Don't let that sweet face fool you—our mom is a rabble-rouser. She's also modest. This paragraph would be longer if Mom hadn't told me: "Soft-pedal the accomplishments. This is really a story about *our family*."—*Susan*

■   ■   ■

So Diane's going to have to brag her up . . .

Black-and-white pictures and colored slides document our childhood. Mom is seldom in the pictures. She is the photographer.

Helene's
Hat Shop

Restyling and Special Orders

232 MAIN STREET

MENASHA, WIS.

After a year at St. Catherine's College in Minnesota, our mother enrolled at Ray-Vogue in Chicago to become a milliner. When she came back to Wisconsin, she opened a hat shop in Menasha. This was her business card.

Former members of the Little Women 4-H Club know how to cook and sew, thanks to Mom and Joyce Misch. The Little Women prove that 4-H is for city girls, too.

Dried flower arrangements and wreaths crafted by Mom adorn the houses of family and friends and Mom and Dad's church. Homemade hoska and oatmeal bread have complemented many a celebration courtesy of our mother.

The Wolf River flows as God intended; Mom helped organize opposition to a proposed dam on the upper Wolf River, and legislation was passed against dams on scenic parts of the Wolf. Mom is a "Caretaker of the River"—there's even a song about her on a CD.

The White Lake Depot project was spearheaded by Mom and friends. They started the White Lake Area Historical Society and raised money to save the White Lake train depot, which was going to be torn down. They had the station moved to a new location and restored it as a museum. Banners representing pioneer families of the area, parades, calendars, and another building that is open year-round are the envy of other historical societies.—*Diane*

■ ■ ■

And Jean gets the last word (Julie is writing about Dad) . . .

Susie, it was turpentine that got rid of Mom's wart. Mom told me it was Grandpa Noffke who gave her that tip. (I didn't know Grandpa ever painted anything.) Mom didn't want to have turpentine on her thumb all the time so she didn't do it, but one spring she did a little painting job around the house and had to keep cleaning her hands with turpentine. That big wart just disappeared.

Mom was a good housekeeper, but she got frustrated by constantly having to do those tedious chores over and over again. She reminded Dad that at least when he built a house, it stayed built. To her it seemed like the only time anybody noticed housekeeping was when it *wasn't* done. When she would get the house and laundry clean, her idea for trying to keep it that way involved hanging us kids naked from the ceiling! Of course she never *did* do that!

Mom sets a very good example for us girls in being a good wife, mother, daughter, sister, sister-in-law, aunt, friend, citizen, church and community volunteer, and Catholic. She always seems to know the right thing to do. So if people tell us that we remind them of Mom, we say, "Thanks," because that's a real compliment.—*Jean*

Copper-tone? Not.

There should be a special patron saint for mothers with multiple teenage daughters.

One summer, our mother, who has very fair skin, bought a Jantzen swimming suit in a blue, purple, and black stained-glass print. (The only swimming we have ever seen our mom do is a keep-your-hairdo-dry dog paddle.)

Every weekday that summer she would change into her new swimming suit and set up a folding aluminum chaise lounge with green-and-white webbing in our treeless backyard. Mom covered her hair with a scarf made into a turban, slathered herself with suntan lotion, tucked her straps into the top of her suit, and lay down on the chaise. Then, she placed one water-soaked cotton ball over each eye. (This drove us crazy.) And our very active mother would just lie there in the sun.

By the end of the summer:

Result No. 1: Mom was exactly the same color as she was at the beginning of the summer. (She could have left the straps up.)

Result No. 2: Her daughters had the very rare opportunity to see their mother "doing nothing."

Result No. 3: The closets were a mess!—*Susan*

Here's proof what a good sport our mother is: she offered us this picture of herself in the same swimming suit—in Florida. (Florida sun didn't work either.)

"See the U.S.A. in Your Chev-ro-let . . ."

" . . . America's the greatest land of all." Dinah Shore belted this song out on her television show and always ended by sending everyone a big kiss: mwah! Chevrolet was her sponsor, but this was more like her show's theme song.

Every fall our local newspaper would run photos and descriptions of the new car models as they came out, and I would cut out the articles and put them on a clipboard. When I was nine or ten, I was fascinated with the new cars, and those cars were really worth a look!

I wasn't the only one of us interested in cars. On the tedious two-hour trip to and from the cottage every summer weekend, we entertained ourselves and our dad by calling out the names and years of cars: "Most-popular-color-'57-Chevy!" (when we saw a dusty rose BelAir).

I have a very dim memory of our old dark green Chevy, but I remember our next car really well. It was a '53 Buick, charcoal gray with a white top and dark red interior—with power windows! (It would be a long time before our parents went for that option again.) Three years later, Dad bought a snazzy 1956 "two-tone" Oldsmobile, bright red and white with black-and-white upholstery, known as The Lemon. There was always something going wrong with it. We were all in that car when a tire blew out, causing Dad to lose control of the car for a while. We were lucky there were no other cars on the highway.

By 1960, Mom and Dad's friends the "Sawicki boys" had a Pontiac dealership and Dad came home with a floor model: a 1960 Pontiac station wagon the size of a parade float, in a bizarre color combination: the car was a metallic copper color (we called it "the hot dog car"), and the interior was an icky green. This was the car we had when I was learning to drive.

The very first time I ever drove a car was in my driver's ed class. The instructor took four of us out, and we took turns driving. When I got into the driver's seat

> "You wouldn't be human if you didn't make a mistake now and then."—Mom

(for the first time ever), our intrepid instructor pointed to a narrow one-lane bridge—it looked like it was meant for a train, not a car—and casually turned around to talk to the kids in the backseat! (If you lived in Omro, Wisconsin, back in the early sixties, you'll know what bridge I'm talking about.) I made it through that skinny bridge without scraping the car, but every single time I drove, I thought I was going to crash.

I was not a natural at this in any way. (Jean was. When I took her out for her very first practice drive, I brought a book to read.) Dad took me practice driving in Menominee Park, and when a flock of birds landed in front of our "hot dog" station wagon/parade float, I slammed on the power brakes so hard that Dad nearly went through the windshield. When I was practice driving with Mom on a back road near our cottage, there was a twig (a branch, maybe?) lying in the road ahead. To avoid throwing Mom through the windshield, I *didn't* slam on the brakes, and that "twig" broke the headlight and mangled its frame. Wrong again.

Finally, I was sort-of-ready to try for my driver's license. The man who took me out for the test had an unlit cigar in his mouth the whole time. The last part of the test was parallel parking. Still chewing on his cigar, the man had me drive down a few streets trying to find a spot to parallel park between two cars, and then he gave up. (I think he was looking forward to lighting that cigar.) This was a stroke of luck for me, because I couldn't have done it—and I passed the test.

For my next birthday, Dad, in what I can only describe as an act of faith, gave me a key chain with an "S" on it—and my very own set of keys for the car.—*Susan*

… and I still have it.

Opening Up Our Closet Doors—in the Sixties

By the time we got to high school, we had learned how to sew. Very simple, short shifts or A-line dresses were in style and very easy to sew, and for little more than a dollar of our babysitting money we could make a new dress for the next Friday night dance. (We had uniforms in high school.) When Julie was about to start kindergarten, we sewed her an entire wardrobe.

After the Beatles became really popular in the United States (I still remember how shockingly *new* their music sounded), the English "Carnaby Street" style began to affect our wardrobes. Mary Quant was a famous London designer at the time, and Diane, Jean, and I each made ourselves Mary Quant dresses from new Butterick patterns. (I looked really terrible in mine.) The dresses had interesting lines and quirky details.

Big fuzzy Mohair sweaters and stretch pants with foot stirrups were in style one of the winters when we were in high school. Another, more "preppy" look was expensive Villager sweaters and matching skirts in beautiful heathery colors with a look of quality we aspired to but couldn't afford. We bought our own clothes with babysitting money (fifty cents an hour), so Bobbie Brooks clothes were more in our price range. It was a good thing we knew how to sew.

One year when Diane, Jean, and I were teenagers, Dad took a chance and bought something different. Mom and Dad were going out, and Dad, as usual, was ready first. He walked into the living room in slim-

Halloween, 1965. Jean is the tall one and Julie is the short one. Only one of these outfits is a costume. Can you tell which one? Hint: "Put an equilateral triangle on my nose." (Jean made both outfits.)

legged, beltless, sleek green pants, and we went into an uncontrollable fit of giggling. One of us managed to choke out "grasshopper pants," and we were hysterical. Poor Dad. We never saw those pants again.—*Susan*

"There's still some wear in that."—Mom

How to Tie a Scarf Like Audrey Hepburn in Breakfast at Tiffany's

Certain people are trendsetters when it comes to fashion. Audrey Hepburn was one of those people. In 1961 she starred in the movie *Breakfast at Tiffany's*. In the film she appeared in an off-white scarf tied in a most unusual way, at least for Oshkosh in the 1960s.

Her large scarf was folded in half to make a triangle. The scarf was placed on her head with the fold framing her beautiful face. Instead of tying the two ends under her chin as most people would do, the ends were crossed and tied in a knot at the back of her neck. The tails of the scarf stuck out from under the knot.

I tried wearing a scarf like Audrey Hepburn did. She could wear a towel wrapped around her head or a sheet draped toga-style—both of which she did in *Breakfast at Tiffany's*—and still look like a goddess. I didn't!—*Jean*

Desperate Measures

Our parents were raised during the Great Depression, which made them Great Improvisers. They taught us how to "make do".

- Out of glue? Mix together flour and water to make a passable paste.

- Is your hair dirty but you can't shampoo it? Sprinkle it with baby powder, rub it around, and brush it out. Okay, so you'll smell like a baby and you'll look like you're going gray—nobody's looking at you, anyway!

- Your hem came loose? A little Scotch tape or a staple will suffice. Note: If you're out of staples, don't use the Paper Staple described on page 170 on a hem!

- Need button thread but only have regular? Dip the whole spool in melted beeswax, let it harden, and you'll have the strongest thread around.

- Outdoor boots lose their waterproofing? Render a little goose fat and keep it in an old coffee can. Brush it on the seams around the sole. As they say, "Like water off a duck's back!"

- Out of apples but want to make an apple pie? Take some Ritz crackers and . . . On second thought, just make something else!—*Julie*

Do-It-Yourself Chocolate Syrup

This is very much like Hershey's (chocolate) Syrup, which still comes in a can like it did back when we were begging our mother to buy it at Kubasta's corner grocery or the Piggly Wiggly supermarket.—*Susan*

1½ cups sugar
1 cup cocoa, unsweetened (the dry powdered cocoa you would use for baking)
½ teaspoon salt
1½ cups hot tap water
1 teaspoon vanilla

Put the sugar, cocoa, and salt (don't leave this out) into a saucepan, and stir to combine. Gradually add the hot water, while stirring the ingredients into a paste.

Cook over medium heat, stirring ocasionally, for around 15 minutes, until you have a thin syrup that coats the spoon.

Remove the saucepan from the stove and stir in the vanilla. Let cool. Store in the refrigerator.

This homemade chocolate syrup can be added to cold milk to make chocolate milk or to hot milk to make cocoa, or it can be poured over ice cream.

How to Make a Folded Paper "Staple"

No stapler? Fold over a little corner of the papers you want to fasten. Make two small parallel cuts or tears in the folded corner. Fold that tab over and—voilà!—your papers are fastened together.—*Julie*

At the Sock Hop

In the summer of 1965, Mom let me start going to the dances that Lourdes High School (where Susan and Diane attended and I would too, that fall) sponsored during the summer months. Since none of my friends or I were old enough to drive, our parents took turns transporting us to and from the dances. We usually had the car crammed full (no seatbelts in those days) by the time we were dropped off at Lourdes.

Once we got there, we paid our fifty cents, went into the gym, and checked out who was there while we took off our penny loafers, summer "tennies," and sandals (after all, it was a "sock hop"; they didn't want us ruining the gym floor with our street shoes) and stashed them under the bleachers.

The girls were dressed in their colorful summer tops or Madras plaid blouses and short culottes, coachman or wraparound skirts, and summer shifts. We better enjoy our dressing freedom now because in the fall when we start going to Lourdes it will be navy blue skirts (that definitely touch the floor when the nuns make you kneel down) and matching bolero jackets with white roll-up-sleeve blouses.

Most of the time there was a disc jockey playing such favorites as "Wooly Bully," "I Got You Babe," "You've Lost That Lovin' Feelin,'" "You Were on My Mind" (my personal favorite), "Love Potion Number Nine," "Hang On Sloopy," "I Can't Get No Satisfaction," and "Ferry Cross the Mersey," just to name a few. Once in a while, a local band would play and it would cost us seventy-five cents to get into the dance.

We danced the night away with the other girls, or if we were lucky, with some of the braver boys. Many of the boys sat up high in the bleachers just watching their less self-conscious peers having a good time down on the dance floor. Sometimes one of them would venture down and bravely ask the girl of his choice for a dance, especially if it was a good slow dance like "Hold Me, Thrill Me, Kiss Me."

It was always a letdown when the gym lights went on full and it was time to head home. A different parent would pick us up and deliver us safely to our homes, where we anxiously awaited the next dance.—*Jean*

Up North

I was blessed to have a good friend, Colleen, near our cottage up north, so there was always somebody for me to play with, but as we got older there were more things in Oshkosh for us to do—which made us want to stay home.

Jean's always been the diplomat of the family. Going to the cottage when we were little did have its simple charms (she will be telling you about those), but as a teenager, a hundred miles away from our friends every weekend from May 1 through Labor Day (trout fishing season)—with no telephone! Need I say more? Sunday night when we came back to Oshkosh we would hear about all the girls our boyfriends danced with at the dance we missed on Friday night.—Susan

On a sunny day at the cottage you could:

- Play under the Oreo Tree. This was a fir tree on a little hill where we often ate Oreo cookies. When the tree had to be taken down, Mom gave us each a piece of it.

- Make fern umbrellas. There were lots of tall, stiff-stemmed ferns in the woods. A bunch of them made a good umbrella.

- Swim at Boulder Lake. Not like the Wolf River: no bloodsuckers, no current, no rocks. A good place to swim, with nice clean sand on the bottom.

- Rock hop along the river shore. Hop from rock to rock and hope not to fall in!

- Eat outside on the picnic table.

Pick a bouquet of wildflowers.

Watch Mom using the wringer washer outside. (*Above the big tub, which worked very much like washing machines do now, there was a wringer: two rollers to squeeze the water out—a primitive "spin cycle." The laundry came out the other side of the rollers, compressed into a flattened wad. "It irons the clothes!" said little Jeanie, who has always been fascinated with how things work.—Susan*)

Jean, Diane, and Julie on Susie's lap at the cottage picnic table. Just behind the picnic table is the worm box. (Check out Julie's leg action!)

Play with the Peters girls. (They lived across the highway.)

Swim in the river.

Look at the stars. Watch for satellites!

Visit our old bus. "Red Rover" was now permanently parked, and rusting.

Make maple leaf chains. Our neighbor, Ruth Buettner, taught us how to do this. You use the cut-off stem to "pin" the leaves together.

Maple leaf chain hats and stoles for all. Ruth Buettner, who taught us how to make them, is at the right.

Go fishing. But remember, you have to bait the hook and clean the fish yourself!

Sleep in the tent.

Wave to passing cars and trucks on the highway. Get the truck drivers to honk their horns!

Wait for friends and relatives to come visit.

Rainy days were another story:

Look at the weird shapes on the knotty pine walls. There's an opera singer and a monkey . . .

Fiddle with the TV reception. This took up a lot of time because the reception was always bad.

Reread old comic books. Pomasl's General Store had a great selection, and Mom bought us each a comic book when we got groceries.

Play cards and board games. Go Fish, Canasta, 500 Rummy, and lots of Monopoly!

- Walk barefoot on the "cookie cutter." The furnace was under the floor in the hallway, and the vent was covered by a large, sharp-edged grid that you had to walk on to get to our bedroom.

- Fight with each other.

Things to watch out for:

- Wood ticks, pine snakes, bloodsuckers, poison ivy, mosquitoes

- All four of us slept in one bedroom at the cottage. Dad built us a bunk bed that fit double bed mattresses. Susie and Julie were the least popular bed partners. When Susie had asthma, her breathing sounded like a mosquito was in the room, and Julie had a tendency to unexpectedly fling an entire leg to the other side of the bed. Oof!—*Jean*

How to Make Maple Leaf Chains

Make sure you aren't allergic to maple leaves (like Susie was).—*Jean*

1. Pick fresh maple leaves (including stems). Snap or cut the stems off at the base of the leaves. You will be using the stems as pins.

2. Overlap one leaf over another leaf as shown in the drawing. Poke the stem into, then out of the overlapping leaves to hold them together.

3. Lay another leaf on top and pin to continue the chain. Connect as many as you need to make hats, necklaces, and bracelets.

How to Remove Bloodsuckers That Are Stuck on You

Horror of horrors: I once stepped into a nest of bloodsuckers in the Wolf River. I yanked off the writhing big black one right away (ick!), but my foot was covered with squirming baby bloodsuckers that were too small to pull off, and I ran up to the cottage for help. Grandma Sanvidge was there and she knew just what to do.

Make a dash for the nearest saltshaker. Open the cap and pour salt on the bloodsuckers. They will shrivel up and . . . "expire."—*Susan*

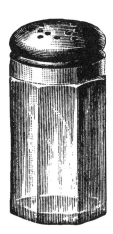

"Rich Sixty's": A Letter from Patsy

Patsy and I sent each other letters when I was up at the cottage, and her letters were always really funny. She wrote just like she talked. The letter below was written when we were both twelve, but it was never sent. Grown-up *Pat* found it and mailed it to me in 2005. Patsy is *so* excited that her spelling and grammar are on summer vacation, but I think that's what makes it sound exactly the way she talked back then. She always had really good grades in English!—*Susan*

Aug. 13, 1960
RICH SIXTY'S

Dear Susie,

I've got quite a lot to tell you. About a week ago I went to Patty Ebner's house to stay for a night. But it turned out I stayed for three nights and three days. Then right from there I went right dirrectly to the Chases and stayed for three days and nights. All this time Mama and Daddy were at the cottage. The after noon they came in town I came home and that day I found out that I had to babysit that night for a five year old little boy who comes from California. I babysat from about 8:00 to 11:30 while his mother and father went to Nancy Davies wedding practice. Before they left they said he might scream a little and that scared me. But after they left he was real good but he went to bed 15 minutes later then he was supposed to because he was watching a show and wouldn't go to bed untill it was over. But I could have shot their dog. They got a sisyfied frence poodle. That stooped dog borked and yiped all night and wouldn't shut up. But guess how much money I got FOUR DOLLERS in cash. But my four dollers is gone already though because we went down town this morning after the wedding and I bought me some school shoes. I like them alright. Their black slipon shoes with gold trim. But I don't care if I'm broke now because I have to go to their house again tonight and babysit again. So I'll be rich before tomorrow again. The little boys name is Tommy and he was at Disneyland. Tonight Mary Lou has to go along and I have to take care of her to. I can have popsikles, vinilla ice cream, chocolate ice cream, and pop. Plus cake and cookies and sandwiches if I want them. Yummy! I sewed some clothes for my Tony doll too. Well good-bye for now.

Love, Pat (PAT)

P.S. Please write back soon and make it a real long letter like this.
P.S.S. Mama got a beautiful royal blue dress. It's lace on top and has a silk under skirt. It almost fits me. Daddy got new shoes. Mama got new shoes. I got new shoes. Mary Lou got to hold the packages.
P.S.S.S. I'm going to celebrate my birthday about the second week of school and am going to have a party with the kids from school. (GIRLS) So you can come.

Grown-up Patsy's Disclaimer: When I found this letter and sent it to Susie forty-four years after writing it, I never thought my poor spelling and bad grammar would end up exposed to public scrutiny. Good thing I wasn't graded on this. Sister Mary Berard would have had heart failure and I could kiss another holy card good-bye. Let's just say my mind must have been racing to download the news of my good fortune while my No. 2 pencil kept experiencing spelling viruses.

I don't think the paragraph had been invented yet.
—Pat(sy)

"The person who dries the dishes has to get that off." —Patsy Lux

"Dearest Wendy": A Letter from Mary Lou

This was a much-appreciated letter when I was stuck up north for a long time, the summer before high school. Mary Lou and I don't remember why she called me Wendy!—*Jean*

Aug. 17, 1965

10:00 Noon
Tuesday

Dearest Wendy,

. . . I went to the dance last night. A new band called the Burgundy's were there. I went with Kathy, Peggy and Judy. On the way there it was raining, but by the time we got there it stopped. We got out in the front of school and a big red sign on the window read Burgundys—75 cents. Mrs. Nitkowski gave us each a quarter [to make up the extra admission cost]. I think it was the biggest crowd they ever had. You couldn't hardly dance without bumping into anyone.

I talked with Jim at the dance. He told me to be sure and tell you he still likes you and he misses you, and you're to write to him. He said he wrote Saturday, and he better get a letter. Someone said Joyce is going for Jim, but I don't believe it. He wouldn't like her because he likes you too much.

Mike Nigl's having a party Wed. (tomorrow), but I'm not invited.

. . . At Kathy Clark's party they broke a flamingo, threw their St. Joseph's statue in the pool and they have to buy two pieces of plywood in their basement because some kids threw darts through the wood.

For some reason I don't think I'd like a party. But I suppose it's all in who you invite.

As far as I know this was the last dance before the yearbook dance. We can't go to the yearbook dance, because the incoming freshmen are having a dance either the 30 of August or the 3rd of Sept.

By the way when are you coming home? This Sunday or a week from then? Last night they announced there's going to be a hootenanny* Mass at St. Pete's Sunday at 9:45. I'd sure like to go. It's for all Lourdes students.

Going back to the Burgundys, I forgot to tell you this. There were 5 guys, they wore burgundy coats with black dickies, black slacks, and beatle boots. Boy they were really good. When they sang "Wooly Bully," they sounded just like the record.

I went downtown yesterday and I got some Dippidy Do. It works good. It makes your hair stay in place longer.

I guess I'm getting short of words but I'll keep writing after you do.

P.S. Please excuse the handwriting you won't be able to read.
P.S. I terribly dislike Terry R.
P.S. Please write back.

Your friend,
Mary Lou

 Mary Lou (Lux) drew this bar of Lux soap next to her name.

*A hootenanny Mass had music played with guitars. It was aimed at appealing to high school and college students.—Jean

Diane's Letter to Jean

As soon as I turned sixteen I got a job at The Continental ("men's clothiers") in Oshkosh. Mom let me stay home to work while the rest of the family went to the cottage. I must have been too cool for capital letters.—*Diane*

(Or maybe Diane was reading too many poems by e.e. cummings?—Jean)

dear jeanne,

how's life in the north woods going? it couldn't be any more exciting than around here.

i bought a real neat camel's hair sweater tuesday. it looks even neater with the pin you made me for graduation. i also put a green cabled sweater on lay-a-way.

real neat camel's hair sweater

Diane drew this on her letter.

i went to the show with degroot last night, it was fun but he's not going to ask me out any more. he's dating a girl from illinois and is really nuts about her. he even went to see her on the fourth of July.

tomorrow is sidewalk day so i suppose i should write my last two letters and get some sleep.

ta ta
your sister
f i f i

p.s. how many dates have you had so far. you probably beat me by a mile.

Susan's Toys in the Attic

Just before I wore my first pair of nylons, I saved up to buy my last doll, a sweet-faced Betsy McCall. I was reluctant to put my toys away. Long gone were my earliest toys, the paper-covered wood blocks with different ears and noses, eyes and mouths on each side for rearranging into funny faces, and the velvety-brown horse with wheels that I scooted around on. My first doll, pink rubber with chewed fingers, was still around, but starting to shrink.

I loved my little Singer sewing machine and used it to make clothes for "Miss Pam." (Miss Pam was a "grown-up" doll with a more realistic shape than the Barbie dolls my sisters would have instead.) I sewed her a stylish wrap coat out of green wool and a black velvet hat and long, fingerless gloves. Miss Pam's boudoir had a piece of green-and-black "marble" Formica for a floor and a couch I cobbled together on Dad's workbench in the garage and upholstered with pieces of our old print bedspreads. Later, I made clothes for my last doll, Betsy McCall, and put the little sewing machine away in its box.

Our Little Golden Books, *The Ugly Duckling*, *The Pokey Little Puppy*, *Little Black Sambo*, and *The Little Red Hen*, were passed on to Julie, but the very best ones of all were still up at Grandma's cottage: *Lucky Mrs. Ticklefeather* (and her pet puffin, Paul) and *The Color Kittens* ("Blue is the door that takes you through . . .").

My two favorite Little Golden Books

The Bobbsey Twins at the Seashore was a birthday present. I read most of that series about Nan and Bert, Freddie and Flossie, and then went on to Nancy Drew. *Clue in the Old Album* was so good that I read it three times in a row, in two days. Nancy's roadster, her girlfriend George, her boyfriend Ned, a clearing in the woods at night, a circle of gypsy wagons, a fire blazing! If our *McCall's Giant Golden Make-It Book* was advertised as "hours of entertainment," it was absolutely the truth.

Stacks of thick Katy Keene comic books (bought on trips to the general store up by our cottage) with wildly inventive fashion designs, and even room designs, sent in by readers—Julie will love these, too. I always thought I would send in designs, but I never did. The stories were never as fascinating as the outfits and backgrounds, but there was quite a cast of characters: Katy Keene (star of the stories, a ravishing brunette); Katy's competing boyfriends, K.O. Kelly (a boxer with red hair and freckles) and Randy Van Ronson (blond, rich); and her little sister, "Sis" (a.k.a. the Candy Kid—all designs for Sis involved candy themes). Katy had a rival/sometimes-friend, Gloria Grandbilt (blond, rich) who was always in a snit about something, and a friend, Bertha (plump, short), who was always sweet. All of the characters wore outfits designed by readers who were given credit in the comic book. There was so much to look at on every page!

The little sewing machine, the pink rubber doll (almost flat now), and Betsy McCall are in my own attic now. Jean rescued *Lucky Mrs. Ticklefeather* and *The Color Kittens* from Grandma's cottage and gave them to me. And, not too long ago, Diane sent me a copy of *Clue in the Old Album*. All of these books are on my bookshelves, not in the attic. When I read them now, they are all exactly as good as they were when I first read them, a long time ago.—*Susan*

How to Make a Yarn Octopus

We all loved the *Make-It Book*. My first attempt at selling a craft project was a yarn octopus. I sold it to Joanne Engeldinger for a dime. The materials might have cost more than that.—*Diane*

You will need:
- a skein of yarn, any kind
- scissors
- felt, buttons, or embroidery floss for eyes
- foam ball or stuffing for the head
- about 2 hours with nothing else to do

1. Wrap the yarn 96 times around the long side of a book. (*Highlights* magazine works great.) Cut the end.

2. Tie a piece of yarn around the yarn at the top of the book. Tie it tight.

3. Cut the loops at the bottom of the book. It looks like this:

4. Position the head stuffing by the tie.

5. Smooth the yarn around the head.

Continued on next page

6. Tie another piece of yarn around the neck.

7. Divide the yarn into eight bunches (each will have 24 pieces) and braid each tentacle.

8. Tie the end of each tentacle braid.

9. Glue or sew on two eyes.

10. Tie a bow at the top of the head if you want your octopus to be a girl.

The Late Sixties

H ave you ever lived in a house with three teenaged girls and a woman going through menopause? I have. Dad bought Breck shampoo in bulk and spent a lot of time out of the house, hunting and fishing. With the Vietnam War and astronauts on our black-and-white TV and rock-and-roll on the transistor radio, I stayed home and wished I was a teenager, too.—*Julie*

Four More Years . . .

As you might have noticed in some of our family pictures, my three sisters frequently dressed in three identical outfits. Was it to save time? It did cut down on shopping time. Was it to save money? Well, you only had to buy one pattern and one long piece of fabric. But if you ask me, I'd guess "squabble control" was Mom's real motivation.

I was born seven years after Jean, so by the time I fit into my sisters' hand-me-downs, the clothes were hopelessly out of date. Thankfully, Mom had fashion sense and knew they would look "Dutchy," so she only made me wear their old pajamas and bathrobes.

One particularly memorable set of clothing clones were red bathrobes. Dark red corduroy bathrobes—ugly, homemade, with unfinished inside seams—one after another. Outgrow the first one? Don't worry: there are two more of those heinous things waiting for you! And when those are through, we'll move on to the next batch of—yes, red corduroy bathrobes in a slightly different pattern. Other kids had fluffy, ruffly, girly-girl pink bathrobes, but never me.

We *loved* those bathrobes! Red corduroy bathrobes, brand-new! Three of them, in three different sizes, to fit a little sister for years (first bathrobe) and years (second bathrobe!) and years (third bathrobe!!) . . . —*Your Big Sisters*

Then there was the summer I started wearing their old shorty pajamas. They were very cute, but storing them in the attic for seven years had taken a toll on the elastic in the bottoms. I remember when I first started dressing myself, I forgot to exchange the shorty pajama bottoms for a pair of regular undies. We went to church and I had to hold them up the entire time.

Occasionally, there would be a laundry mishap

and Mom would wash one of my teen sisters' fashionable wool sweaters with the regular wash and it would shrink to just my size! Too bad, Susie!

Really good hand-me-downs came in large grocery sacks brought by Grandma's beloved housekeeper, Lucille. Cile's niece, Nancy, was a couple of years older than me and had exquisite taste. She cleaned out her closet a couple of times a year, and I was the lucky recipient of her largesse. No more pedal-pushers for me—I'm wearing something mod!—*Julie*

Julie, this is your big sister Susan speaking. I have some bad news for you: Nancy was a few years older than me! I'm glad to hear you enjoyed the brown denim jeans, the jodhpurs, and the white T-shirt with "Nancy" written in candy canes as much as I did, even though those mod clothes were at least twelve years old . . . and double hand-me-downs. Maybe she had a little sister?—Susan

"Nancy did *have* a younger sister," says our mother. (. . . *and she didn't have to wear hand-me-downs because her big sister gave her old clothes to us.*)— *Diane*

Dad holding Jean, Susie (with doll), and Diane in a blue coat and snow hat.

. . . and here's Julie in the same blue coat and hat about eight years later.

If You Eat Your Bread Crusts . . .

When I was a child in the 1950s, there was a popular saying (mostly among parents) that if you ate your bread crusts, you would get curly hair. I guess I must have eaten lots of bread crusts, because in those days I had a head of thick, naturally curly black hair.

My mom liked my hair color because it made it easy for her to pick me out in a crowd of other kids. In those days, the citizens of Oshkosh were predominantly of European descent with mostly blond or brown-haired children, so I stuck out like a sore thumb.

My hair's natural curl posed a challenge for Mom. For my sisters, a cut of the bangs and a trim of the ends kept them looking neat. As I got older, my hair got even thicker and curlier (like a bushel basket), and that type of haircut just didn't work for me. Since Mom wasn't sure just how to cut my hair to look its best, she took me to a couple of professionals. One of them was the beautician wife of

Curly-haired Child Jean

Dad's favorite plumber. Watching her cut my hair must not have provided enough tutelage, because Mom also took me to the barbershop in the beautiful old Athearn Hotel in the heart of downtown Oshkosh (which has since been torn down).

As the barber cut and shaped my hair, every time his scissors touched a certain spot on my neck, it resulted in an involuntary kink in my back—which made me jerk. The barber probably thought I had "ants in my pants" or something. I must have been a more willing subject than most of his other little clients, though, because he gave me a nickel for being good. I really didn't think I deserved it, but what kid could turn down free money?

Certainly not me!

Mom eventually did start cutting my hair again. During my freshman year in high school, Susie even took a shot at cutting my hair. She scared me, though, when she cut one side of it (to look like a fellow Lourdes student's cute, naturally curly hairdo) and then wasn't sure how to get the other side of my hair to look like the first half. I think I started growing it out after that!

Surfer Girl Jean

During the '60s, the "California look" became popular. Long, straight, and blond was the style for hair. That was not exactly what a girl with medium-length, curly black hair wanted to hear. I decided not to bleach my hair, but thanks to orange juice cans used as rollers, I did get it straight. If the weather was damp or humid, Mother Nature had her way and it frizzed back up.

From who knows where I got the idea of using gelatin as a straightener. This must not have been too successful, because I also resorted to a commercial straightener. When that method was rejected, Susie and I even tried ironing each other's hair!

Flower Child Jean

In the '70s, while I was in college, the "flower child" look was in, and frizzy hair was popular. Finally, a look I could easily do! Dad wasn't too thrilled with my new hairdo because it made me look like a hippie.

I'm not driven by the latest style anymore, and my black hair has turned to silver (after a few years of dyeing it). The curl has relaxed to nice waves, which I'm very grateful for when I hear how much my friends pay for a permanent. I've even learned to cut my own hair. All things considered, I'm really glad that I ate my bread crusts, because now I love my easy-to-care-for curly hair.—*Jean*

"... and Don't Let the Bedbugs Bite!"

Going to sleep in the Sanvidge house is different from going to sleep anywhere else. Who else do you know who always opens the window at night—even if it's just a crack—even if it's 20 below?

Who else has thick, hand-tied wool quilts with an extra pocket of fabric tacked to the top? Grandma Noffke called the addition a "breather" and said it extended the use of the quilt top.

What other kids knew how to execute "hospital corners" when making a bed? Grandma Sanvidge, a former practical nurse, taught us how. No sissy fitted sheets for us back then—we used two flat sheets!

Can't find the ever-necessary Kleenex in the dark? Grandma Sanvidge kept tinted tissues in her bedroom so they would show up against the white sheets.

Remember "Sleep tight. Don't let the bedbugs bite!" and "If I should die before I wake . . ."? How were we expected to sleep after hearing that? Well, comfort yourself with the knowledge that your scapular will keep you from plummeting to the depths of hell before morning. G'night!—*Julie*

I'm Going on a Diet

By the time I got to high school, dieting had become popular. Weight Watchers was newly established and our neighbor, Carolyn Jones, was following the plan. The girls in my class were always trying to take off a few pounds before the big dance. My interest, or obsession, with dieting and makeovers began in kindergarten . . .

The annual Christmas program at Emmeline Cook Elementary School was scheduled for an evening the week before Christmas. Our class was going to sing

"Rudolph the Red-Nosed Reindeer." The chubbiest boy in the class would wear a Santa outfit and the rest of us would wear our holiday best for the program. That boy managed to get chicken pox, and the next chubbiest was ME. I had to take his place! Mom practically had to drag me there that night, and the rest is history ...

One summer, Susan and I went on a boiled egg and soda cracker diet. Jean didn't participate. To fill all the time we were not eating, we counted Jean's calories ... as she ate—a heartless running tab as follows:

Jean eats a:

potato chip: 10 ...

potato chip: 20 ...

potato chip: 30 ...

sandwich: 330 ...

soda: 480 calories!

This diet did not make us skinny. It made us unpopular in our house. Ah, the cost of beauty.

The arrival of *Seventeen* magazine was always inspirational. We mixed egg yolk facials and tried cucumber eye treatments. We did the recommended spring, summer, and fall exercise regimens. We shopped for all the right outfits and accessories. This got Susan a position on the Jeffrey's teen board. (Jeffrey's was a store with really neat clothes.) I knew we were on the right track.

In my sophomore year, Dad and I tried the new "grapefruit diet." Eat a grapefruit before every meal and only eat meat and vegetables. This worked great. Unfortunately, this was Dad's annual Lent diet. Easter came; Dad was done. You can't do this diet alone, especially with Easter baskets and Hughes' chocolates in the house.

I have tried a lot of fad diets, joined the ranks of nearly nude women weighing in at Weight Watchers, and kept Diet Coke in business for a lot of years. . . . Now every Christmas, Jean and her husband dress up as Mr. and Mrs. Santa Claus, and they don't seem to mind. Can I quit now?—*Diane*

From the Kitchen

Broiled Grapefruit

Grapefruit, as many as you need (Each grapefruit makes two servings.)

For each grapefruit *half*, you will need:

    2 tablespoons light brown sugar
    ½ tablespoon butter! (cut into pieces)
    1 maraschino cherry

Cut grapefruit in half (as shown in drawing). Cut out the pithy center, remove seeds, and cut the sections away from the membranes. Cut the grapefruit away from the rind all around. Place grapefruit halves in a shallow pan, cut-face up.

On each half, spoon the brown sugar onto the surface, press down with a fork, and place butter pieces across the surface.

Broil about 4 inches from the broiler flame (on "Lo") until the sugar is bubbling all over, about 5 minutes or so. (Some of the sugar will run off the edges.) Place a cherry in the center of each grapefruit half, and serve while still very warm.

On the Job with Dad

When we had a day off from school, I was thrilled for more than just the obvious reason: it meant I could beg Dad to let me go to work with him. More times than not, he said yes.

The experience started with a walk across busy Bowen Street to Noffke Lumber (run by Uncle Hank and Uncle Jim after Grandpa retired), where Dad's truck sat overnight so it could be loaded with lumber and supplies for the next day's work.

After saying hello to my uncles and the people who worked for them, and often Grandpa, too, because he still enjoyed being there, it was off to the job in Dad's big red GMC dump truck. I loved riding in that truck with my dad. It was usually a short ride to the job site, since many of the well-built houses that our dad, Neil V. Sanvidge, built were in the same northeast section of Oshkosh we lived in.

Dad told his customers if there was anything wrong with the job he did for them, they should tell him and he would fix it—which he did. Because Dad built his reputation on quality and fair prices, and stood behind his work, he had many repeat customers over the years. Many of his customers became his friends, which I think says a lot about Dad.

On the job, Dad's crew (his brother Keith; childhood friend Billy Judkins; Bob, Roy, or Larry Carpenter; for a while our cousins Tommy and Johnny) were all so nice and friendly toward me. I would keep busy picking

Dad's big red truck. We loved to "tap dance" on the bed of the dumper because it made so much noise.

"If you make too much money, it's coming out of someone else's pocket." —Dad

up nails and sorting them (no air-gun nailers for them!), sweeping the floor, or fetching things.

The time passed quickly, and before you knew it, it was time for the morning coffee break. We all sat down to eat a donut or sweet roll with lighthearted conversation to go with it, and then it was back to work. When I was older, I actually got a summer job (with pay!) working for Dad. My work included all the tedious jobs that nobody else wanted to do: scraping plaster off the floors after the plasterers were done; screwing down subfloors with a ratchet driver (no power drivers then) until the palms of my hands blistered and peeled; and sanding wood trim all day with an electric sander. (My arms tingled for hours afterward from the vibration.)

Ah, then there was lunchtime, one of the best parts of the experience. If I was lucky, it would mean a stop at a nearby restaurant, where I could choose anything I wanted from the menu. You can bet that dessert would be chocolate cream pie, if they had it.

Back to work again in the afternoon. Sometimes Dad and I would head out to a privately owned dump site on County Y to dispose of scraps and construction debris. Once we spotted some discarded silver-plated items. There was a baby cup, a beautiful lacy-looking plate, and a small rectangular plate. I still have those things and cherish them as mementos of those wonderful days "on the job" with Dad.—*Jean*

Our Hero

When we were dating, Dad would tell us before we went on a date that if any guy did anything that made us uncomfortable, we should call him, and no matter where we were or what time it was, he would come get us! I think the truth is that all Dad had to do when faced with one of his daughters' suitors was stand up straight with his six-foot height, his strong muscular arms sticking out of his white T-shirt, and look the poor guy right in the eyes, no need for words. Dad's size and demeanor spoke volumes!—*Jean*

For most kids our age, their heroes were Mighty Mouse ("Here I come to save the day!") and Superman ("faster than a speeding bullet"); for us, it was Dad. We love this picture. It was taken when Dad was an MP in the Philippines during World War II.

To the Rescue

When I was a freshman in high school, Susie was a senior and Diane was a sophomore. It was great having two sisters who had paved the way for me. They gave me advice and made sure I didn't buy elevator passes. (There was no elevator in Lourdes High School.)

When I was seventeen, my date, Jonathan (who was eighteen), and I joined some friends at Old Town, a bar and restaurant on Main Street in Oshkosh. (At that time the legal age for drinking beer was eighteen in bars that served only beer and soda pop, and twenty-one in places that served hard liquor.) As I don't much care for the taste of beer and I wasn't of legal age to drink it, I was there (honest, Mom and Dad!) for a late-night snack and the companionship of our friends Carl and Nancy (both eighteen).

We were having a really fun time when Susie and her boyfriend showed up. She didn't say much, but she shot me one of those "What are you doing here?" looks. I decided that now would be a good time to leave. Good thing that I did, because the place was raided by the police about twenty minutes later, and all the underage kids were hauled down to the police station, where their parents were called to come get them! Whew! That was a close one. (Thank you, Susie!)
—Jean

Jean's Ideal Christmas Shopping Trip: Oshkosh in 1965 (Part One)

Disclaimer: This is Oshkosh in 1965, but Jean never had enough money in her pockets to keep shopping for so long. If she had, this is exactly what she would have done. I can vouch for her shopping stamina.—Susan

Petula Clark's "Downtown" is playing in my head as I hurry down Bowen Street to Custer Avenue to catch the Bowen and New York bus to downtown Oshkosh. I can't forget all *my* worries—I have to figure out what to buy for Christmas presents! I hop on the bus. I have to remember to pick up the snow flocking spray Mom asked me to get for that spindly Christmas tree we got.

Before I know it, the bus lets me off at the corner of Main Street and Washington Avenue. I stand there taking in all that Oshkosh ambiance . . . I'd better get going!

I glance up at one of the taller buildings in Oshkosh, the First National Bank.

A postcard showing Main Street in Oshkosh in 1958. The buses look the same as the ones we took in 1965, and most of the stores were the same, too.

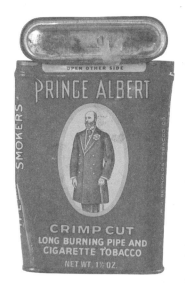

Good thing I keep my money in this old tobacco can Dad threw out, to remind me what kind he likes.

In it is the office of our favorite dentist, Dr. Weinzierl, and his friendly receptionist ("Mix me an alloy"), Joan. If I'm lucky, when we go to see him Mom will agree to walk up the three flights of stairs to Room 310, since the elevator makes me sick. (It stops, but my stomach doesn't.) Fortunately, today I do not have a dentist appointment—lucky me! I round the corner and head north on Main Street.

As I step on the doormat of the Osco Drug store, the door opens for me—no hands! Think I'll check out some English Leather cologne for you-know-who, some Jean Naté for Susie, a bottle of Chanel No. 5 (or Christmas in July?) for Mom, and, for sure, some Wind Song ("Helps You Stay on His Mind") . . . for me.

Next door is Pallin's Photography Studio. Mr. Pallin takes photos for Lourdes High School. I'll have to ask Susie if he's the one who took her graduation photo. *(Yes, he took that picture. Do you think that over-the-shoulder pose was my idea? No.—Susan)*

I decided to make a stop at the Exclusive Record Mart. With a little assistance, I decide to get the 45 rpm record "Keep on Dancing" by the Gentrys for Susie (she loves dancing); "King of the Road" by Roger Miller for Dad; "You Were on My Mind" by the We Five for Diane (one of those "to her for me" presents—I love that song); and "You've Lost That Lovin' Feelin'" by the Righteous Brothers . . . for me. Good thing that salesman was so helpful.

A quick stop at Derkson and Sons tobacco shop to check out pipes for Dad. Don't see one I like, so a can of Prince Albert Pipe Tobacco will have to do, and a copy of *Mademoiselle* magazine . . . for me.

One of my favorite of all the shops in downtown Oshkosh—The Caramel Crisp Shop—is calling to me. If I'm lucky enough to go to the dentist on my own, this is where I head afterward for a big bag of delicious caramel corn (which fortunately tasted better than it smelled in the shop, or was that just me?). Sorry, Dr. Weinzierl, to mess up that great teeth-cleaning job you did. "Just a little bag of caramel corn for me, please."

I glance in the window of the Glass Restaurant to see if any of my friends might be there. With the booths (which my friends and I prefer) it is hard to see. Oh well, no time to visit, anyway.

I zip past Hilda's Women's Apparel and Bridal Shop, home of the Lourdes uniform. At least it's where we are measured and fitted and where we pick them up. But no need to stop today. Upstairs Mr. Litjens has a tailor shop. I don't need him, either, since I'm the tailor at our house.

(to be continued . . .)

Lourdes Homecoming

Homecoming was a big deal at Lourdes High School. It was usually held the first or second week in October. Weeks before, confident boys would ask their favorite girl to accompany them to the dance. Boys who weren't so sure of getting a yes often waited until the last minute. Lucky the girl who was asked early; she would have plenty of time to find (or sew, in our case) suitable outfits for the parade, game, and dance. Invariably, if you had a wool outfit, it was sure to be Indian summer and you would sweat your way through the weekend.

Voting for the Homecoming queen and a girl representative from each class (for prom, we voted for prom king and a boy representative from each class) was done the week before and was announced the Monday of Homecoming week. The boys on the court were the guys who just happened to have asked the winning girls to Homecoming. Being on the court was a big deal. The closest we Sanvidge sisters came to reigning was when Susie was Senior Girls Representative, runner-up to Queen Mary Jane.

Each girls' homeroom was paired with a boys' homeroom to build floats for the parade. (At that time Lourdes High School was actually two separate schools: the girls' school was located upstairs and was run by the School Sisters of Notre Dame, while the boys' school, on the main floor, was run by the Christian Brothers.) Each group of float-building students chose a theme, came up with a clever slogan, and found a suitable large hay wagon or trailer to build the float on. (If your group was lucky, you had a student from a farm in your group!) Most important, a tolerant parent offered a site for constructing the float—hopefully not too far from the parade route. We had less than a week to put together our masterpieces. We probably helped keep Kimberly Clark in business with all the Kleenexes we gathered together to make "flowers" to stuff into the chicken wire frames of our float structures.

In 1968, Diane's senior year, a Thursday night bonfire was held behind the school to get us revved up for the big weekend. That year Lourdes was playing De Pere's Abbot Pennings, and a large letter *P* was burned at the stake. The cheerleaders led us in cheers.

Friday was Spirit Day. The nuns let us girls dispense with wearing our usual navy blue uniforms so we could dress in our school colors of red and white. An all-school pep rally was held in the gymnasium. The girl cheerleaders and boys pep club led the classes in a competition for the Little Brown Jug—the winners were the class that could cheer the loudest. The pep rally also featured the presentation of the queen and the senior class skit.

Saturday, the big day of the weekend, started with an early morning Mass in the decorated-for-the-dance gym. It didn't have quite the turnout the rest of the events did, but the queen and her court were expected to be there.

The Homecoming parade through downtown Oshkosh was next at 11:00 a.m. Hopefully the float you worked on so hard made it to the parade in one piece, and if your group was lucky it won first place like the Alice-in-Wonderland-themed float "We'll Paint Their Tulips Red and White" that Susie's homeroom worked on in 1965. Besides the twelve floats, there were pep club boys and cheerleader girls riding on tandem bikes rented from the Schwinn Bicycle Shop (better known as Vern's Cycle Center). (*Later my husband and I bought Vern's house and the attached former bicycle shop and turned the shop into a rec room. —Diane*) Convertible cars with their tops down, sporting clever slogans, had the Homecoming court members perched on the tops of their backseats as they paraded down Main Street.

Certainly the whole of Oshkosh didn't show up to cheer on the Lourdes

There were "go-go dancers" on every episode of *Hullabaloo*, a popular TV musical variety series in the mid-1960s. Those dancers-in-a-cage inspired this float in the Lourdes Homecoming parade.

students, but most of the proud parents and younger siblings (dreaming of their Homecoming days to come) sure did. And some of the faithful alumni were probably there at the parade and the game to cheer on their alma mater. (If the alumni were there, we were too busy to notice.)

The big football game was next on the agenda in the early afternoon. At that time Lourdes did not have its own football field, and all of their home games were played at the Jackson Street Athletic Field. Most of the students were decked out in red and white to cheer on the Lourdes Knights. The school band was there to play for the team. The players were introduced and the game began. At halftime the Homecoming court was introduced, and the queen gave a heartfelt speech. Often halftime was capped off by a Knight in shining armor riding his steed across the field to the cheers of the crowd. It was also tradition to release red and white balloons. The game continued after halftime; with any luck the Knights won, and there was a little time to go back home to clean up, rest, and dress up before you headed out to eat with your date.

The dance was the icing on the cake. Some of the girls wore huge mum corsages (only one mum per corsage) with dangling wooden football charms. Oftentimes, half the petals fell off before the coronation. The usual Homecoming dress was wool with a modest hemline, high neckline, and long sleeves. At least with an outfit like that a fellow could find a suitable spot to pin that big corsage on! Most of the boys wore sport coats, dress pants, white shirts, and ties. We danced to the music of a local band.

The culmination of the dance and weekend was the crowning of the queen. The previous queen got the honor of placing the crown on her successor's head. At least we know that *one* of the alumni was at Homecoming!—*Jean and Diane*

How Not to Enjoy Homecoming

My senior year at Lourdes High School, I volunteered to be in charge of decorating for the Homecoming dance—what was I thinking?! It was a big responsibility and a huge job to make a gym look like something other than a gym. As I remember, we tented the whole gym with red crepe paper streamers. The part I liked best was making the backdrop for the queen and her date. I designed a gridded backdrop of four-inch shiny red circles that were spaced two inches apart and held together with wire. Those circles were given to us by Grandpa Sanvidge. They were scraps from his Oshkosh Cutting Die business that he thought we could use, and we did.

My hardworking crew and I decorated the night away and headed home as the milkmen were out on their early morning routes. (I can't believe Mom let me do that!) I got so little sleep that I really wasn't able to enjoy the parade, game, and dance very much because I was way too tired!—*Jean*

Jean's Ideal Christmas Shopping Trip: Oshkosh in 1965 (Part Two)

Jean is still Christmas shopping . . .

I hurry past the Overflow Tavern.

I decide to stop at Thom McAn Shoes to see if they might have a pair of shoes I can wear with the dress I am planning to sew for Christmas. No luck.

I hear "Jingle Bells" coming, I think, from Wilson Music and Appliance. A strange combination of merchandise, I muse, as I enter the store to check on a harmonica for Dad. I find just what I want and can afford.

Back outside, I pass by Barney's Tip Top Tavern and duck into The Main Surplus Store at the corner of Main and Merritt, where much of their stock

is military surplus. I want to check out the peacoats—too expensive for my babysitting budget. I do find a pair of mittens . . . for me.

Back on Main Street, as I wait to cross to the west side of the street, I glance north to the marquee of the Raulf Theatre to see what's playing. *The Sound of Music.* Wonder if Rose would want to go.

Across from the Raulf is the Magnet Bar and Pool Hall. I don't think my mom would approve.

When I finally get to cross the street, I stop in at Julie Ann Fabrics. I check out the Simplicity, McCall's, Vogue, and

Butterick patterns for a possible Christmas dress. Those Mary Quant patterns that Butterick has are so cool, but I'm not sure. Maybe Susie would design one for me; then I'll look for a pattern that's similar. I'll have to try hard to get it done before Christmas so I'm not hemming it in the car on the way to Mass like last year. I don't think Mom liked that.

A little window-shopping at Callinan's Shoe Store saves me a trip inside. Next, I pass by Race Office Supply, home of the best art supplies in Oshkosh, and it's on to Kitz and Pfeil Hardware to pick up the Christmas tree lights that Mom wants.

As I walk past the Time Theatre, I notice that *My Fair Lady* is playing. I bet Mary Lou would enjoy that.

I dash past The Lullabye Shoppe, grateful to have outgrown the sizes in that place.

Next door at Jeffrey's I'm sure to find something for Susie. She is serving on the store's teen advisory board, which I guess is a way for the store to find out what fashions young women her age are interested in. Susie even got us tickets to one of their style shows held at the new Oshkosh High School auditorium. Little vials of Famé perfume were handed out—and unfortunately opened up. I got a banger of a headache thanks to that perfume! Is that Mr. Hirschberg, the owner, over there?

Great! There are a couple of colorful watchbands I think Susie would like, and a gold circle pin for Diane, and a poorboy sweater . . . for me.

Back outside, Britton's Walk-over Shoe Store is another chance to window shop. Looks more like Mom might find what she wants among all those Hush Puppies.

I'm bound to find something for Julie at J.C. Penney.

"It's better to buy expensive shoes for everyday and cheap shoes for dress-up."—Mom

Wow! I didn't know that The Continental had its own labels!

If not, I can just ride the escalator a few times. It's the only one in Oshkosh, and the thrill hasn't worn off yet. I luck out and find a pair of socks for Julie. I remember she doesn't like "puh-ple," so I get white ones, with ruffles around the top, and a pair of slipper socks . . . for me.

I pass by Apparel Arts, a women's clothing store, where a quick glance confirms there is nothing I am interested in.

At Lucille's, I find a pair of stretchy gloves I think Mom might like, and— shock and surprise—a pair for me, too.

I breeze past Krumrich's Jewelers, since it's way beyond my puny budget, and Ahern Men's Clothing. Lucky for me, Dad's more of a Joe's Sport Shop kind of guy.

I pop into The Continental to say hi to Diane, who works there. Great place to work, with all those guys (working and shopping)! And how fun to put the money in the wire basket and send it up to the cashier on the little mezzanine. Darn, I missed her. She went to lunch, with the boys, at the Raulf Hotel.

At the House of Cards and Cameras, I purchase a 1966 calendar for Mom and Dad and a new diary . . . for me.

(to be continued . . .)

It's All Beige and Cocoa Brown

When our green living room carpet and magnolia-patterned drapes (a woodsy look that always attracted our wild rabbit, Peppy, when he escaped his box) started showing signs of wear, Mom decided it was time to redecorate. Our colorful, cozy fifties living room was about to enter the sleek and modern sixties (sort of).

Diane and I think that Mom might have been influenced by the "modernizing" of St. Mary's Church. The church we knew so well after all those hours of staring at every detail—all the meticulously detailed, richly colored carvings, little clovers and rosettes, the huge columns with what looked like clusters of breasts on top—everything was washed over with what looked like thick cream. (Whoever did the painting saw the same thing we did: there were now gold "dots" in the center of each "breast.")

The soft red, textured wallpaper on the east wall of our living room was the first to go, and the whole room was painted light beige. Our threadbare carpeting and tattered "jungle curtains" were replaced with beige-and-brown-flecked "broadloom" carpeting (twelve-foot-wide strips, as wide as our living room; no fraying edges like our old narrow-strip carpeting), and shiny beige fiberglass drapes with a discreet woven texture, *very* sleek and modern, and light as air. The new drapes (which looked nothing like Fiberglass insulation; no warnings not to touch them, unless our hands were dirty) wouldn't fade like our old ones did, a big selling point with Mom. The worn, but still scratchy, cocoa brown frisé davenport and matching chair were sent to the upholsterer and came back covered with brand-new . . . cocoa brown frisé. It did look a *little* different: the old-fashioned fringe on the bottom was replaced with an up-to-date skirt with box-pleats at the corners.

There was only one spot of color left in the room—a side chair, upholstered in rust. Mom told us if you did a room in neutrals you could always add color later, but she never did.

Before: Our two grandmas in the Bowen Street living room. (Our friend Tommy is playing with Diane's musical bells.) There's a wall of soft *red* wallpaper, a *turquoise* lamp base, *green* carpeting, and *multicolored* "jungle curtains." The "Chinamen" statues on the TV (not shown) have *chartreuse* hats. Grandma S. is on the *cocoa brown* chair that matches the couch.

After: Diane (wearing the Mary Quant dress she made) is sitting on the *cocoa brown* davenport in front of the *beige* fiberglass drapes. (That's the pillow from the den.) Can you see why we wanted to decorate?

One weekend, Diane, Jean, and I had the house to ourselves. (We all had part-time jobs by this time and couldn't go up to the cottage as much.) The moment Mom, Dad, and Julie left the driveway, we all had the same thought: let's get some *color* into that living room!

We found a patchwork-print throw pillow in the den that had a few scraps of color in it, and got some Indian throws from our bedrooms to drape over all that cocoa brown. We scoured the house for anything colorful. Scraps of fabric, vases, magazines . . . Jean remembers that even an orange rubber ball looked like it would add a little personality to the room. Then we looked at those plain, plain beige walls.

I was in my first year of college (living at home), an art major taking a figure-drawing class with a nude model. I had a stack of big charcoal drawings that would really spice up those beige walls, so we taped some up. By the time we were done with that room, bongo drums and beatniks would have fit right in.

Oh dear. I seem to have forgotten Mom and Dad's reaction to our redecorating for some reason, but after *that*, I'm pretty sure we had to stay at Grandma's every time they went to the cottage without us. I do remember Mom showing some of my charcoal drawings of that nude model to Grandma Noffke, who asked me:

"Is her hair red?"

"Yes."

"She's renting our house on Powers Street."—*Susan*

Bermuda Pink

After years of hearing us whine about her conservative color choices, Mom let us choose the paint color for our old pale green playroom—if we would paint it ourselves. We chose "Bermuda Pink," an intense coral. Diane and I were just finishing the first wall when she turned to me and said, "Is it getting hot in here?"—*Susan*

Jean's Ideal Christmas Shopping Trip: Oshkosh in 1965 (Part Three)

Jean is *still* Christmas shopping . . .

Across Algoma Boulevard, I'd better check out Nobil Shoes to see if they have any interesting shoes in their window. No, guess not.

Think I'll pop into Newberry's for a Bun candy bar. This shopping is making me hungry!

A couple of doors down, in the windows of the Big Shoe Store, I spot a cute pair of shoes. I'd better check them out. Inside, the salesman greets me and I point out the pair of shoes. I'm not sure what size I wear, so I sit down and the salesman brings over his special shoe stool. He has me stand up and put my shoeless right foot on the special size gauge contraption (must be a better name for that thingy, but I don't know what it is). Size 7M. With that, he disappears behind a curtain and, after checking the ends of rows and rows of boxes, he comes back with my size. I try on the right shoe and, just to be safe, the left also, and walk around a bit. Now all I have to do is talk Mom into letting me get them and hope they still have my size when I come back.

At Kresge's dime store, I purchase a box of Christmas cards to send out to my friends, a copy of *Glamour* magazine for Susie, a Colorforms set for Julie, and a tube of lip gloss . . . for me.

Back out on Main Street, I pass by Carl's Shoe Store and take a quick glance just to make sure there aren't any shoes I like better than the ones at the Big Shoe Store . . . guess not.

Dashing across High Avenue, I avoid looking at the windows of Mangel's Feminine Apparel. All that red underwear—how embarrassing! I quickly duck into Johnson Hill's (a department store). I hop on the elevator and tell the operator, "Second floor, please." I quickly check out the Women's Department, just in case I might see an outfit I like. No such luck.

Back out on the street, I stop on the corner by the New American Bank. Glancing to the west, I notice the big hole left by the demolition of the beautiful Athearn Hotel where Mom used to take me for haircuts. I hear that the New American Bank is going to build there. Across the street the Grand Opera is looking not-so-grand.

I cross Pearl Avenue and pause to look at the pretty Christmas window display at Anger's Jewelry Store, but I'm sure everything in the store is way out of my budget range. Sherwin-Williams Paint Store—where Grandpa Sanvidge gets the rolls of Scotchlite for his Oshkosh Cutting Die business—don't need to go there. Rodat Jewelers, also too expensive, but I'd better check out O.A. Haase Shoe Store, just in case.

Back on the street, I quickly breeze by Meyer and Schmidt Jewelers and Barnett's Photography Studio, both sharing the same building with the Cushion Billiard Hall, Agrell and Brueske Interior Decorators, Seckar Electric (I think the Frank Seckar who goes to Lourdes is related to them), and Buehler Bros. Meat Market before stopping in at the Hobby House to pick up some glitter to make bottle-cap hot pads for presents. I find just the green I was hoping for.

Next door is the D & B Furniture (skip that); Dunham-Fulton Gun Co. (no thanks); WG&R Furniture (don't need to go in there); Vern's Cycle Center (nope), and I'm already to Marion Road.

(to be continued . . .)

"Hey! What's That?"

If you beamed yourself back in time and walked through our house on Bowen Street, you might find some slightly odd items. Some things were a little different when we were growing up . . .

In the Kitchen

- Metal ice cube tray: Fill with water. Spill, spill, spill on the way to the freezer. Pull the lever to release the ice cubes. (*If you can unstick your frozen fingers from that metal lever!—Jean*) Pick up the released ice cubes from the floor. Use the remaining three ice cubes for your drink. Repeat.

- Joy dishwashing soap: No squirt bottle; measure one capful to do dishes.

- Tiny loaves of Wonder Bread: A supermarket giveaway.

- A butcher-wrapped package with string around it: Your meat purchase is in there!

- A package wrapped in newspaper: The garbage is in there, all set to be carried out to the metal garbage can by the garage.

- Campfire marshmallows packed in boxes: Bring these back!

- Home-cooked chocolate pudding sitting on the counter with wax paper to prevent skin on top: Susie still finds skin.

- Three-tiered rolling metal utility table: Watch out for the toaster cord!

- Pig fat cooking in a cast-iron pan on top of the stove to make cracklings: Not heart healthy! (*Our mother notes that she was actually "rendering lard." Those delicious cracklings were just the leftovers in the hot liquid lard. —Susan*)

- Telephone without a dial: You would just pick it up and tell the operator, "Stanley 95, please."

- "Chicagos": Rectangular, frosted sweet rolls from LaFontaine's Bakery for six cents. These are called long johns now and sell for sixty cents.

In Dad's Office ("The Den")

- Scotch tape: In a red plaid *metal* dispenser.

- Scripto pen: The pen with the real ink cartridge!

- Funk and Wagnall's Encyclopedia: This was picked up volume by volume from the Piggly Wiggly. A yearbook was available every year to keep the set current.

In the Living Room

- Taxidermied red squirrel on a log: We loved this thing. Some kid may have eaten what it was posed to be eating. (*"That squirrel was the only thing I ever shot," says our mother. "It was an acorn."*)

- Human television control: Hurry up and invent the remote control!

In the Bathroom

- Pink Ban roll-on deodorant: This was a very slight improvement on B.O.

- Sudden Beauty Face Mask: Bye-bye, blackheads. (Oh no! Someone's at the door!)

- Cloth baby diapers, diaper pins with sweet plastic animals at the ends, plastic "diaper pants," and the diaper pail: Do I smell ammonia?

- Air-Wick (fifties-style): This was in a glass bottle with some sort of felt folded over a wire, steeping in bright green goo. You used the wire as a handle to pull it up. It smells so fresh in here!

- Maybelline mascara in the slide-open box with the little red brush: For your eyebrows and eyelashes. First you wet the brush with spit . . .

- Doughnut-shaped face protector: Like a little umbrella, with your face under it and all your hair sticking through the hole, so Mom wouldn't get shampoo in our eyes.

- Bobby pins, brush rollers, pink foam rollers, net roller cap cover-up: We had a neighbor who washed her hair, then wore the rollers until the next shampoo, or so it seemed.

- Yardley Oatmeal Soap: You can still buy this.

- Sunbeam hair dryer with plastic cap: State-of-the-art!

In the Basement

- Gallon bottle of Breck shampoo: We can save money here.

- Cream rinse concentrate: You put a tablespoon of this in a measuring cup, added water, and poured it over your hair. It always cooled off too much before you were ready—especially in the basement! Dad didn't want the bathroom drains clogged, so we washed our hair in the basement laundry sink. It was c-o-l-d down there.

- Wooden pop cases: For hauling all those bottles of Jic Jac home from Harra Beverage.

- Cardboard freezer containers: To freeze the garden excess.

- Wood storm windows: These were stored in the basement and washed by the entire family in fall. The rags were Dad's old T-shirts.

- The roll-away bed: Covered with an old bedspread . . . Nightmares of becoming a human sandwich! (*One time a friend slept over and we got to laughing so much that the bed folded up on us. Our legs and arms were sticking out the sides—like a sloppy sandwich—and we were laughing too hard to get out.—Susan*)

- Canvas-topped folding camp stools: Not too comfortable.

- Army cots: Spare "beds." Not too comfortable.

In the Back Door Hall Closet

Mitten clips: These would ensure that you would never lose your mittens—and would not be able to get them on.

Wool skating socks: With pompoms on the back!

Rubber boots: With zippers and fur tops that you put *over* your shoes.

In the Bedrooms

Wallpaper made of newspaper put up with scotch tape! Who did this? (*Jean, the decorator! And I thought it was a great idea. Red, orange, and pink stylized flowers cut out and pasted on top of the newspaper, very "mod."—Susan*)

Paper dolls: Hours of fun, but we had to pick up our "schnitzels."

Coloring books with tracing paper: Now even Diane can draw.

The game SKUNK. We actually never figured this game out, but we liked that the dice had a skunk in place of the "one" dot.

Freezer wrap and brown paper bags: To transform into book covers. Better yet were the white book covers that St. Mary's handed out on the first day of school.

"But Mom, we'll clean it up when we're done."—Susan, Diane, Jean, and Julie when leaving "schnitzels" all over the floor

How to Make a Book Cover Like We Did in Grade School

At St. Mary's, our textbooks were passed on to students the next grade down, and the nuns insisted that we protect them with paper covers. Being supplied with special blue-on-white St. Mary's School book covers is such a dim memory that it must have lasted one year only. Freezer wrap and brown paper covers were the norm.

For a very long time *our* textbooks were covered with foil-coated Sealtest Fudge Swirl ice cream box wrapping, taken from a mammoth roll salvaged from somewhere by our dad. We used the paper white side out, but we always knew that bowl of delectable Fudge Swirl was underneath.—*Susan*

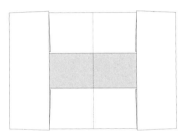

1. You'll need a piece of paper about 2½ inches bigger than your open book—on all sides. Lay the book open on the wrapping paper.

2. Close the book. Fold the paper in on the top and bottom so that about an eighth inch shows above and below the top and bottom of the book.

3. Hold the spine of the book down on the center of the folded paper, and bring the left side up and fold in over the front cover of the book. Bring the right side of the folded paper up and fold in over the back cover.

4. Slip the book covers into the end pockets you have made with your folds, and the cover will stay on your book.

- Head scarves:—Fold these into a triangle and tie under your chin.

- Petti-pants:—Self-explanatory (if you know the word *petticoat*!)

- Cotton ankle socks that slide down in your shoes, or the improved model: swirl-it socks—Jean loved these.

- Black stirrup stretch pants from Janus Sales:—Bend your leg and it bounces right back!

In the Closet and the Junk Drawer

- Green Stamps: These would be thrown in the kitchen junk drawer until one of us would gather all the stamps together and fill the book so we could get our premium.

- The Sweater Shaver: Get rid of those pills!

- Electrolux canister vacuum cleaner: A good friend of Mom's!—*Diane*

How to Make a Flibber

We made these when Julie was a little kid and we were in our early teens. We found flibbers in a book called *How to Make Flibbers, Etc.: A Book of Things to Make and Do*, by Robert Lopshire. You are going to want to make one right now to carry in a parade, decorate your room, or bonk your little sister on the head when she's not looking.—*Diane*

1. Find a newspaper. (Make sure it's one that everybody has already read!)

2. Lay three full sheets of the newspaper lengthwise on the floor, overlapping each one about 6 inches over the one before it.

3. Roll the newspapers up starting on the short side. (Roll about the size of a paper towel tube. Put a rubber band (or tape) around the roll so it doesn't unravel.)

Continued on next page

4. On one end of the roll, use a scissors to make four cuts about one-third of the way in.

5. Put your finger inside the cut end of the roll and hold on to one piece. Pull gently and keep pulling . . .

"Girls! I wasn't finished reading that paper yet!"—Mom

Jean's Ideal Christmas Shopping Trip: Oshkosh in 1965 (Part Four!)

Jean. *Jean!* JEAN!! Time to go home!

Looks like nothing but taverns in this block. Take your pick: The Little Flower Tavern, and across the street, Jack's Bar and Uncle Bud's Tavern. Can't imagine why there are so many taverns! There are a couple of paint stores, Seefluth's and Gehrke's, and a couple of furniture places: Sharpe Furniture and, across the street, Home Furniture.

Time to cross Main Street again and head to Joe's Sport Shop. (I heard Mr. Bleckinger owns this store. His kids are really into tennis. He probably opened the store so he could get their equipment wholesale.)

Gee whiz, more bars! Schaefer's Bar, Del Rio Bar and Lounge, and the Empire Bar. At least there are a few shops for the ladies: Ada's Hat Shop, Vicky's Bridal, and next door, Alden's Catalog Store. (I do like to see something before I buy it.)

Finally—Joe's Sport Shop! Wonder if Dad would like this fancy spinner? Think I'll take a chance.

Wow, I'm getting hungry. As I pass Oshkosh City Cab and the Greyhound Bus Station, I notice their Terminal Restaurant—guess I'm not that hungry! Did they really think over all the definitions of the word *terminal* before they came up with that name?

Crossing Otter Avenue, which becomes Pearl Avenue once you cross Main Street, makes me wonder whose idea it was to also have Waugoo Avenue become High Avenue; Washington become Algoma; and Merritt become Church. Probably somebody who spends a lot of time in all those Main Street bars!

I go past Mueller-Potter Drug, a good place to get a delicious Smith ice cream bar, but not today—it's too cold. I also pass by Kline's (another department store)—I must be getting tired. Oh no! More red unmentionables in the windows of Christensen Style Shop (all lingerie), better known as the "Mountain Shop" to us Catholic school girls. With all those red undies, it looks like they're dueling it out with Mangel's across the street!

At this point, I have one thing on my mind—food! The lunch counter at Woolworth's will do just fine. I dash past the Oshkosh National Bank and Zimmerman's Haberdashers (whatever that is!).

With a brief pause in front of Oaks Candy Shop (chocolate can stop most girls in their shopping tracks), I make up my mind to come back for dessert on my way back to catch the bus—real food first. I'm in luck. There are plenty of empty stools since I shopped right through the lunch hour. Marcie takes my order and brings me a big juicy hamburger, French fries, and a 7UP. Two bites into my delicious burger and I realize, oh no, it's Friday! A good Catholic girl shouldn't be eating meat on Friday. Oh well, what is it Grandpa Noffke likes to say? "Nobody ever went to hell for what went into his mouth, more likely what came out of it." And besides, I can't waste this—there are a lot of starving children in the world, and I don't want to be one of them!

Pleasantly full, I head back to Oaks to satisfy my sweet tooth with a couple pieces of English toffee. (They're good, but I still think Hughes' are better. But Hughes' shop in the basement of their house is way over on Doty Street, and that's too far for me. Sure hope Uncle Keith brings us a box of Hughes' Chocolates again this Christmas.)

Nibbling away, it's back to Waugoo Avenue to catch the bus. It's not quite time for the bus, so I can check out Ruth's International Gifts, which shares a space with Fox Valley Travel Agency. I think Mom would like this little cup and saucer. She sure is nuts about dishes. I can't imagine why!

There are still a few minutes left as I backtrack past Richard's School of the

Dance. Just enough time to check out The Fatima Shop. Maybe I can find a new statue of Saint Joseph the Carpenter (Dad's patron saint). Poor Saint Joseph has gotten knocked off Dad's desk so often that Mom's having a hard time gluing his head back on! Darn. The statues all cost more than I have left, but I can afford this little ornament for Julie.

It's time for the bus! As I settle myself down in the back of the bus ("Downtown, don't wait a minute for . . .")—flocking spray! I forgot that flocking spray Mom asked me to get!—*Jean*

The End!

Hey, Jean—Julie says she has some money she can lend you . . . —Susan (See pages 67 and 68.)

How to Make Bottle Cap Hot Pads for Christmas Presents . . .

. . . when you've spent most of your money on things for yourself .

You will need a circle-shaped piece of pine or another soft wood so your nails will go in easily, about 8 inches across (but you could make smaller ones). The nails should have heads (so the nailed-down bottle caps won't pull off) and be short enough that they won't stick out the bottom of your piece of wood. The bottle cap hot pad in the illustration uses 37 bottle caps and nails— but have plenty of spares (especially if you can't find a little upholstery hammer that will fit inside the bottle caps without smashing them).—*Jean*

1. Spray paint the wood (I made mine dark green).

2. Starting in the center of your wood circle, nail on bottle caps (the kind that come on beer bottles), crinkled-edge, open-side up. (Make sure the nails you have won't come out the other side of the wood circle.)

3. When you have covered your wood circle with bottle caps, spray paint it again. You can even sprinkle on some glitter like I did to fancy it up.

I remember making Christmas wreath hot pads: rings of wood (painted green) with bottle caps (spray-painted red) nailed in a single row around it. But Jean didn't have enough time.—Diane

Moving Out and Up

In 1971, The House We Grew Up In Most had a For Sale *sign on it. Diane got married and I moved out—and soon Jean would be living in an upstairs apartment at her friend Rose's house near her college classes. Dad was building a new house next to our cottage up north for himself, Mom, and Julie.—Susan*

© Toburen Photography, Antigo

... and we grew up. We're in front of the fireplace in the new house Dad built up north, and it's the early seventies (left to right: Diane, Susan, Jean, and Julie, with Dad and Mom in front of us). Lester Grose, who did the masonry on our fireplace on Bowen Street, laid the fireplace in this new house, too. Julie was still living with Mom and Dad ...

After Mom, Dad, and I moved to Langlade, we would return to Oshkosh to visit and usually stayed at Grandma Noffke's house. I always slept in the larger bedroom at the front of the house, the room that Hank and Jimmy shared while growing up.

On one visit, Mom had me sleep in her old room, in her old bed, instead. It was right across from Grandma's sewing room. As Mom kissed me goodnight, she shared an interesting and heartwarming tidbit of our family's history: her Grandma Schroth *died* in this room, in this very bed! G'night!—*Julie*

Dad, the Natural-Born Engineer

It's too bad that Dad didn't get to go to college to study architecture or engineering because he had a head for numbers, an eye for square and level construction, and an inventive and improvising nature that he inherited from his father. Dad received some formal training in basic woodworking, building techniques, and drafting at a local vocational school, but much of what he accomplished can be chalked up to this: Dad was a natural-born engineer. Let me give you a few examples.

In the early seventies, Dad was asked to build a house that had an unusual and new architecture for the time—it had a massive laminated beam that ran the length of the roof and supported the entire house. When finished, the house would look something like an upside-down ship with a large expanse of windows angling out and up two stories in the front. He took the job, studied the plans, and sat down with his crew at the kitchen table. He and Fritz Buettner, another natural-born engineer, and the other men thought about the different ways they could accomplish the task, and they finally settled on rigging some scaffolding and using some block and tackle assemblies to gradually hoist the beam. I'm sure they had to solve other problems along the way and carefully plan the order of their work. The result was breathtakingly beautiful, with the huge windows looking out over a beautiful Northwoods scene.

On the home front, Dad was always fiddling with his fireplace and wood-burning setup. He never liked the draftiness that came with a fireplace and set out to eliminate it. He built the fireplace with the ordinary Heatilator inside, something you buy and build a fireplace around that better captures the fire's warmth and sends it out into the room. He made a rectangular opening in front of the fireplace—it was about the size of a brick—and fabricated a little sheet metal cover that fit snugly into the opening. The opening was the end of a small duct that went to the outside of the house. When the fire drew air from outside, it didn't draw air from the room. Voilà! No drafts. He also made it so the little door could be propped up, directing the air flow under the fire. Voilà! It worked like a turbo bellows when you wanted to start a fire.

Safety was an issue with Dad, too. He installed glass fireplace doors he could close when we left or went to sleep. But he didn't like how the fire looked all stirred up behind them or the flimsiness of the doors, so he drew up a plan for steel doors and took it to Mike Klimoski, an expert welder. Mike made the doors, and Dad installed them and painted them with stove black. Fort Knox doesn't have doors as solid and airtight as these.

He was concerned about chimney fires, too. He heated the house with wood and took care to monitor the tarry buildup in the chimney. We had a chimney fire in there once that scared the bejeezus out of us, and he didn't want it to happen again. He took some sheet metal and fashioned an internal sleeve to fit snugly down the chimney. He'd periodically slip it out, burn off the creosote, and put the liner back into the chimney.

Getting enough firewood together to heat the house, heat the garage (72 degrees all winter!), and keep the fireplace stoked took a lot of work. At first Dad cut up the tornado-downed trees on the Highway 55 property he and Mom owned. Then, over much protest from Mom, he started to cut down standing trees. About the time his friend Roy Carpenter was tragically killed while felling a tree, Dad decided to go a safer route and began ordering eight-foot-long logs from one of the Popelkas. He cut them up right next to the driveway.

Now, how to split that much firewood? Hmmmm.

Dad and Marv Zaddack, yet another natural-born engineer, figured out a way to build a wood splitter to attach to the back of Dad's tractor and operate off the tractor's hydraulic system. It worked like a charm, but neither one was completely happy with it, so they built a second, improved one for Marv's tractor.

Dad liked everything he made to be perfect. We often heard from both our parents that old adage "Good—Better—Best, Never let it rest, Until the Good is Better and the Better is Best." Dad lived it! He had built a huge garage for us with our house up north—it held two cars, his tractor, my little Volkswagen Beetle, a large workshop area, and a generous wood supply. He had a simple barrel stove that kept the garage toasty all winter and, as a result, melted all of the snow and ice off the vehicles.

That was a problem. Clumps of filthy ice, puddles of muddy water, salt deposits, gravel—all of it ended up on the garage floor. If it were me, I'd probably just mutter under my breath as I cleaned it up. What did Dad do? When he had a few days between summer jobs, he had his crew break up the garage floor and he replaced it, adding plenty of drains.

In later years, Dad tackled smaller problems like unlocking car doors remotely. Picture this: Mom and Dad are somewhere. It's time to leave. Dad, the gentleman, goes to get the car so he can pick Mom up at the door. The car doesn't have automatic locks. Dad can't maneuver himself over to the other side of the bench seat to undo the lock. Voilà! Dad creates a little pole with a handle on one end and a hammer-claw-shaped dealie on the other side. With this nifty device, he can open the lock from his own seat. Sometimes he took this kind of thing a little far, carving costly black walnut into replacement pieces for cheap little clothespin hangers that had broken—but by then he had a lot of time, and wood, on his hands. He also tried rigging up various Rube Goldberg–like devices to outwit the squirrels and keep them from the bird food. Some entailed spikes made of nails, some slippery sheet metal. All of it looked like hell, and the squirrels still got the bird food. That's about the only thing at which he failed.

A while ago, my boyfriend was up on a tall ladder painting his house. He was trying to hold on to the ladder, hold a paint bucket, and paint at the same time—a precarious situation, indeed. I observed this for a few minutes and went into the house. I cut up a wire coat hanger, bent it into a strong hook, and ran it through the rim of a very large plastic pop cup. I took it outside, filled it with paint, and handed it up to him. He promptly hooked it to the ladder rung and was thrilled with it.

Am I a natural-born engineer?

Not by a long shot.

But every once in a while, I feel like a little of Dad's ingenuity has rubbed off on me.—*Julie*

Dad's folding rule

Under the Influence

Some fragments of childhood become part of who you are; others are reasons for rebellion; and some come back to haunt you—in a good way.

Etched into my brain . . .
Think long and hard before you throw anything away. You could make something out of it. You might need it. You could fix it. Someone else could use it. What else could I use this for? Maybe if I change the buttons . . . ? I still have my eighth-grade winter coat.

Do it yourself; figure it out. You don't want to have to depend on others to do what you could do yourself, do you? This has led to some pretty bizarre accomplishments among the sisters: carving missing chair spindles, repairing washing machines, cutting down trees, pouring a cement stoop (with little pebbles on the top) . . .

First do your work; then you can play. This one is indelibly etched into my brain. A refrain of "You're supposed to be . . ." runs around in my head, until I'm actually doing what I was supposed to be doing.

Always have a Kleenex in your pocket. Allergies do run in our family (but this rule turns out to be pretty obnoxious on laundry day).

Go to the bathroom before you leave the house. Or some little piggy will be "crying wee, wee, wee, all the way home." An *excellent* rule.

Make the bed when you get up. Will you make your bed at any other time? This is more important than you think. It helps you start the day feeling organized, and it makes you a lot less likely to cave in and take a nap. Who wants to make the bed twice?

Jean has three rules to add:

No boy jobs, no girl jobs. Growing up in a family of all girls, they were just jobs (or chores), and you did them. I was the lawn mower and the snow shoveler.

Put things away when you're done with them. Thanks to this lesson there have been very few times that unexpected company has seen my house messy.

Do your work first; then play. This is a lesson that all of us can thank both Mom and Dad for. *(Does this sound familiar?)*

There'll be some changes made . . .
Scissors in every room! We could never find a pair of scissors in our house when we were growing up—that's why we had to use Dad's hidden nail scissors. I now have a pair of scissors in every room. Every single room.

A full bag of chocolate chips in every batch! After teasing Mom about this for years, imagine my horror when I discovered that for years, I have been using half the amount of pecans called for in the Tollhouse chocolate chip cookie recipe.

Use the good dishes anytime you want! Why not? There's too much to do when you have company. You don't even get to see the dishes until your guests leave, and then—they're dirty.

No bedspreads! Cuts bed-making time in half. No bedspread falling on the floor.

Stay inside on a beautiful day anytime you want to! "Girls, it's a beautiful day. You should be outside." I think that's the reason I love rainy days so much.
—*Susan*

It's Amazing We're Alive!

There have been lots of changes in what is called "safe" since we were kids in the fifties and sixties . . .

The baby car seat we had hooked over the back of the car seat with two metal prongs and had a steering wheel to keep the baby occupied. There was no seat belt to hook it onto, so that was it. Just those two prongs.

Infants could ride in a "car bed." Ours was navy plaid and could be folded up. You just laid it on the backseat.

Mom had her own version of automobile safety. She reached her right arm out like the safety bar on an amusement ride at every stop to protect the front-seat passengers. When you got bigger, you sat, lay, or crawled wherever you wanted . . . no seat belts to keep you from roaming all over the inside of the car.

Almost everything liquid came in glass bottles. Milk, shampoo, deodorant . . . Glass-bottled shampoo was hard to hold onto with slippery hands. Jean once dropped a half-gallon glass bottle of milk and it shattered all over the kitchen floor.

When straight hair was in style, Jean and Susan took turns laying their heads on the ironing board, spreading their hair out, and ironing each other's hair, right up to their ears.

School paste smelled minty and delicious. Kids couldn't resist. If paste was meant to stick things together, what did it do to your insides?

Jean used the leaves of a sedum plant in Mom's garden to make frog-belly whistles. When we tried to find out what kind of sedum she used, we discovered that the sap of many sedums causes respiratory distress. Wheeze! Wheeze!

If you scraped your knee, you could count on Mom to clean the wound and paint on Mercurochrome with the little glass dauber. Yikes! That stings! AND there's mercury in it. Isn't that poison, Mom?

You know those little silver pastry-decorating balls? We ate tons of them. Now we find out you're not supposed to eat them. (What's with that? Use them for decoration on your cookies and pick them off???)

We once spent an entire day playing with a *fascinating* little ball of mercury from a broken thermometer.

See? It is amazing we're alive!—*Diane*

These Things Make Us Happy . . .

The sun sparkling on water, the sound of a distant motorboat, the way coffee smells on a cold morning. All is right with the world. My brain has been sent back to heaven-on-earth: Grandma and Grandpa's cottage in Three Lakes.—*Susan*

A big bowl of popcorn. Reminds me of all those times Dad made popcorn for all of us. We'd even have it for supper sometimes on Sundays; now it's one of my favorite lunches.—*Jean*

Quilts. "Sweet dreams!" On all our beds at home, we had thick, but light, hand-tied wool-batt quilts, just like Grandma Noffke had at her house. Cool on the outside, warm on the inside—and comfortable year-round. We went with Mom and Grandma to Courtney Woolen Mills in Appleton to buy the big rolls of batting, and we watched as Mom and Grandma sandwiched the puffy batting between layers of printed cotton (on a frame that filled most of the living room), and held the layers together with little yarn ties. (I have quilts like this in my own house, too.)—*Susan*

Ice cream. We loved it when Grandma made homemade ice cream at family reunions. We begged to stop for cones at Pierre's Grocery in Leeman on the way to the cottage. We craved black cows and root beer floats from the A&W. We walked blocks to get to Leon's Frozen Custard across from the fairgrounds. We bought Drumstick frozen cones at the Piggly Wiggly. When Mom offered us a pedestrian dish of "just plain old vanilla" *ice milk,* we grumbled, but we always ate it. A curl of vanilla on a dish of apple betty, a scoop to make our pie "à la mode," on a cone, or in a dish—it is all delish!—*Julie*

Making multiples. I get this from Dad. I can't seem to make just one of anything. Knit ten pairs of socks; line them up in a basket. Crochet twenty baby hats; pose them on every wine glass I own. Make thirty jars of raspberry jam; line them up on the counter. Dad made fishing nets and at one time had 1,500 of them hanging in neat rows from the basement ceiling.—*Diane*

Red plaid. You will be taken care of and have everything you need. Red plaid was like a theme song for our family. Mom made matching red plaid dresses with green rickrack for herself and her daughters, and a shirt out of the same plaid for Dad. (She never sewed much after that.) I started grade school with a red plaid lunch box filled with food from home. Dad's Pendleton wool shirts, school bags, dresses, winter scarves, thermoses, Christmas ribbons, pleated skirts, Dad's wool Jones caps—all red plaid.—*Susan*

Picking a bouquet of flowers. When we would travel up north to our cottage on Fridays, the first thing we had to do was unpack our suitcases and put our clothes into the drawers that Dad built for us right into the wall of our cottage bedroom. The next thing I always did, because I wanted to, was pick a bouquet of wildflowers. I still enjoy that time outdoors picking flowers. And what a treat it is to have them in the house.—*Jean*

Fixing things. I was very blessed that I inherited my father's and his father's mechanical skills. In fact, when I was in high school, I got a 99 in mechanics on my Kuder Preference Test! It gives me a really good feeling when I can make or fix a lamp, repair a leaky faucet, replace the inlet and flapper valves on our toilet, get our lawn mower going in the spring, make rain collectors out of rubber storage bins, repair our refrigerator, or rewire our electric stove.—*Jean*

Lilacs, lilies of the valley, peonies. School's out. Every May, kids would bring bouquets of flowers from their backyards to put in front of Mary statues in every classroom. The fragrance of lilacs and lilies of the valley filled our grade school, as warm summer air wafted through the windows—very soon we would be cleaning out our desks. By the time Grandma Noffke's peonies were out—so were we!—*Susan*

A fragrance from Grandma's garden, buttery popcorn on a rainy Sunday afternoon, the sound of a distant motorboat . . . *What do you remember?*

How This Book Came About

It all started with a family cookbook the four of us wrote as a Christmas present for our parents in 2003. Our parents were delighted with *Never Let Anyone Go Hungry at Your House: Sanvidge Family Recipes and Food Memories.* While we'd been "stirring up the past" with our childhood recipes and food memories, all sorts of memories that had nothing to do with food had come back to us and our mother said, "Write more stories!"

We wrote the first batch of what we called *Oshkosh Stories: It's Not All About Food* for Christmas 2004 and presented our stories to Mom and Dad in a small ring binder. We wrote a second batch of stories (with holes punched to fit the binder) for Mom's birthday in 2005. Meanwhile, our cookbook had made several more trips to Kinko's, and people were telling us we should have it published. We sent in a book proposal to the Wisconsin Historical Society Press, and not long after we received a letter that our book was being considered. Our cookbook was accepted for publication a few days after our dad died.

We wrote our last batch of *Oshkosh Stories* for our first Christmas without Dad, in 2005.

In late November 2007, our cookbook was published as *Apple Betty & Sloppy Joe: Stirring Up the Past with Family Recipes and Stories,* and we went back to the stories we had never made into a book. We couldn't help adding a few more, and our *Oshkosh Stories* became the book you are holding now.— Susan, Diane, Jean, and Julie

"Do they still make Geritol?"
—Diane, in 2005

A Thank-You to Our Editor

We'd like to raise a toast (with hefty Wisconsin supper club Manhattans) to the intrepid Kate Thompson, acquisitions editor at the Wisconsin Historical Society Press, for seeing worth in the self-published family cookbook we sent her, for helping us to transform the stories we wrote into this book, and for her expertise and unfailing enthusiasm throughout the process of getting both books ready for publication.

About the Authors

Susan Sanvidge is a freelance graphic designer in Chicago. Diane Sanvidge Seckar is a journeyman electrician and co-owner of Seckar Electric in Winneconne, Wisconsin. She also designs and makes crocheted hats and purses. Jean Sanvidge Wouters is a homemaker, seamstress, and volunteer in Winneconne. Julie Sanvidge Florence is the director of the Lebanon Public Library in Lebanon, Ohio. Their first book, *Apple Betty & Sloppy Joe: Stirring Up the Past with Family Recipes and Stories*, was published by the Wisconsin Historical Society Press in 2007.

The Sanvidge sisters: Diane, Julie, Jean, and Susan

Index

also games; playing
outside
redecorating, 209–211
red plaid, 89, 236
Red Rover, 9–10, **9**
religion, 139–143
rings, lost, 11
Romie (family friend), 73
Rover. *See* Red Rover
Rowe, Beverly, 34
Ruby, Jack, 145
rules to live by, 232–233
rye bread, 114–115

saddle shoes, 93
safety standards, 234–235
Santa Claus, 76–77
Sanvidge, Bert, 109, 111
Sanvidge, Cliff, 109, 113
Sanvidge, Helen Noffke
(Mom): after big storm,
10; on buying shoes,
207; with daughters,
66; Diane on, 160–
161; doing yard work,
6; at Easter service,
140; Jean on, 161; at

Langlade house, **227**;
memories of family
home and, 5–6; in mid
sixties, **159**; pin curls
and, 30; redecorates
house, 209; rye bread
recipe, 114–115;
style of, 89–90, **89**;
sunbathing and,
162, **163**; Susan on,
159–160; takes Susan
practice driving, 165; at
Three Lakes cottage, **57**
Sanvidge, Keith, 195
Sanvidge, Ken, 109
Sanvidge, Linda, 109
Sanvidge, Millie, 109, 110,
112–113, 135
Sanvidge, Neil V. (Dad):
after big storm, 10;
commonly used phrases
of, 121–123; dating
and, 197; desk of,
118–119; with Edith
and Roy Carpenter,
122; goes on grapefruit
diet, 193; houses built
by, 2–7; ingenuity of,

228–231; memories of
family home and, 4–6;
as MP in Philippines,
197; in new house,
227; Red Rover and,
9–10; smoking and,
120–121; in snow, **189**;
style of, 89, **89**; takes
Susan practice driving,
165; with television,
85; wears "grasshopper
pants," 166–167;
working with, 195–196
Sanvidge, Ruth Safford
(Grandma Sanvidge):
at Powers Street home,
2; bedtime and, 192;
Christmas trees and,
72; in living room, **210**;
memories of, 79–81;
Myron Floren and, 34;
with television, **85**;
visits Bowen Street
home, **79**
Sanvidge, Susan: on Apple
Fritters recipe, 63; on
Aunt Millie's Southern
Fried Chicken, 112;

189; on sock hops,
170–171; on Steal the
Bacon, 16–17; style
of, **92**; takes piano
lessons, 136–137; at
Three Lakes cottage,
57; on working with
Dad, 195–196; writes
in Diane's autograph
book, 39
Wrchota, Tommy, 149

yarn octopus, 185–186,
186
Young, Loretta, 90

Zaddack, Marv, 230
Zuelke, Mr., 36